THE
GOOD NEWS
FILE

THE GOOD NEWS FILE

HOPE FOR A MODERN WORLD

D. LYNN MICKLESON, MD

Copyrighted Material

The Good News File: Hope for a Modern World

Copyright © 2022 by Good News Publisher. All Rights Reserved.

No part of this publication may be reproduced, stored in a retrieval system or transmitted, in any form or by any means—electronic, mechanical, photocopying, recording or otherwise—without prior written permission from the publisher, except for the inclusion of brief quotations in a review.

For information about this title or to order other books and/or electronic media, contact the publisher:

Good News Publisher
www.goodnewspublisher.com
goodnewspublisher@mtaonline.net

ISBNs:
978-1-7378703-0-2 (softcover)
978-1-7378703-1-9 (eBook)

Printed in the United States of America

Cover and Interior design: 1106 Design

There are no mistakes,
no coincidences.
All events are blessings
given to us to
learn from.

~ Dr. Elisabeth Kübler-Ross
(Swiss-American psychiatrist)
(Author of *On Death and Dying*)

. . .

Possibility Thinker's Creed:
When faced with a mountain
I Will Not Quit!
I will keep on striving until I climb over,
find a pass through, tunnel underneath,
or simply stay and turn the mountain
into a gold mine, with God's help!

Dr. Robert Schuller
(American theologian)

*This book is dedicated to my two kids . . .
Faye and Travis,
my loving and supportive parents and family,
my friends, and my colleagues in Alcoholics Anonymous.
We are all on a journey of learning, growth, and healing.*

Credits

All efforts have been made to attribute proper authorship to the material in this book. Any questions or concerns, please contact goodnewspublisher@mtaonline.net

~ THE AUTHOR

Table of Contents

	Introduction	xvii

2.0 WISDOM 1

2.1	Desiderata	3
2.2	Wisdom	5
2.3	The Station	10
2.4	Law of Unintended Consequences	12
2.5	The Seeds of Character	14
2.6	A Quiz	16
2.7	Some Thoughts for a Vital Life	18
2.8	Laws of Life	20
2.9	The Four Agreements	22
2.10	An Ethical Will	24
2.11	Instructions for Life	26
2.12	Dealing with the Burdens of Life	28
2.13	How Do You Live Your Dash?	30
2.14	A Blueprint for Living	33
2.15	Lao Tzu	34
2.16	Abraham Lincoln	38

2.17	A Zen Story	43
2.18	Civilization	45
2.19	Why Is There Hatred?	46
2.20	On Slavery	48
2.21	Ben Franklin	49
2.22	Education	52

3.0 SPIRITUAL WELLNESS 55

3.1	Talk to the Potter	57
3.2	Spirituality	60
3.3	Ascension	67
3.4	Helping Others	68
3.5	Law of the Garbage Truck	69
3.6	The Law	71
3.7	The Privilege of Life	73
3.8	Love—The One Creative Force	75
3.9	A Creed for Those Who Have Suffered	77
3.10	A Christmas Wish	79
3.11	Ten Rules for Being Human	80
3.12	On Being Hurt	82
3.13	I Am Thankful For . . .	84
3.14	Your Spiritual Journey	86

4.0 SERVICE 89

4.1	Acts of Random Kindness . . .	91
4.2	Acts of Service	94
4.3	My Twenty-Foot Swath	97

TABLE OF CONTENTS

5.0 SUCCESS 101

5.1	The Admiral's Lessons	103
5.2	Success	108
5.3	Mistakes	126
5.4	Success and Failure	129
5.5	Boldness	142
5.6	A Commencement Address	144
5.7	All I Ever Needed to Know . . .	147
5.8	Attitude	149

6.0 MEN AND WOMEN 151

6.1	On Marriage	153
6.2	A Male Fairy Tale	166
6.3	Togetherness	167
6.4	Marriage	170

7.0 TRAVEL 173

7.1	The Tourist Ten Commandments	175
7.2	On Wilderness	179

8.0 RELIGION 183

8.1	One Solitary Life	185
8.2	The Lord's Prayer	187
8.3	The Eternal Truths	188
8.4	Reincarnation	190
8.5	A Daily Prayer	193
8.6	Forgiveness	194
8.7	Gandhi's Faith	196

8.8	Prayer of St. Francis	197
8.9	What It's Like in Heaven	199
8.10	Angels	201

9.0 BUSINESS SUCCESS 203

9.1	Fail Your Way to Success	205
9.2	Business Success	208
9.3	A Letter to Corporate CEOs	217
9.4	Formula for Growing Rich	219
9.5	Creativity	220
9.6	Viking Laws	221
9.7	On Military and War	224
9.8	The Stock Market	233

10.0 HOPE 243

10.1	Adversity	245
10.2	The Mountain of Problems	247
10.3	Perseverance	250
10.4	If	255
10.5	Inspiration	257
10.6	Courage	260
10.7	Cherokee Indian Legend	262
10.8	The Donkey	264
10.9	Only a Person Who Risks Is Free	266
10.10	Today	268
10.11	On Youth	270
10.12	Keep On Going!	272
10.13	Anyway	304

TABLE OF CONTENTS

11.0 HEALTH 307

11.1	Physical Health	309
11.2	Mental Wellness	311
11.3	A Prayer for Those Who Live Alone	313

12.0 HUMOR 315

12.1	Humor	317
12.2	Stress Diet	323
12.3	Responsibility	326

13.0 ALCOHOLICS ANONYMOUS 329

13.1	Alcoholics Anonymous	331
13.2	Why We Were Chosen	335

14.0 PARENTING 337

14.1	My Own Parenting	339
14.2	On Parenting	344
14.3	Things Our Parents Meant to Tell Us . . .	347

15.0 FINAL THOUGHTS 351

15.1	Believe in Yourself	353

16.0 ABOUT THE AUTHOR 359

ACKNOWLEDGMENTS 361

1.0 Introduction

This is a book about hope.

The year 2020 has been a difficult one for the entire world—a true *annus horrobilis*. The COVID-19 virus has killed millions, and tens of millions have either lost their jobs or had their businesses closed. And the end is not yet in sight. If there's ever been a time for hope, it certainly is now.

I am a born optimist. Some people say I overdo it and am too helpful and cheery and optimistic, but I've found it to be the best way to lead my life. Given the problems and negativity in this world, I figure it's better to err on the plus side than the negative.

Now, more than ever, there are a lot of unhappy people in the world. We live in a complex and ever-changing world. Our lives and time are consumed by family, jobs, friends, hobbies, and, of course, Facebook. Our modern cell phones have more computing power than the entire U.S. space program in the

THE GOOD NEWS FILE

1960s, and the internet can be an endless source of fascinating information. Both Facebook and Google can consume vast amounts of our time. Often we find ourselves inside our phones more than actually talking to people.

This is a book about finding wisdom and happiness in the 21st century. Wisdom comes from surviving the tough times. It is neither a romance nor a mystery novel but a collection of inspirational stories and quotes from many sources—famous authors and writers, books, friends, and personal experience. It's about life and everything in it—jobs, marriage, children, friends, failures, addiction . . . and most important about the disasters and calamities that come our way. The good times are easy but it's the tough times that test us and force us to grow into better, wiser, and more loving human beings. The greater the pain and struggle, the greater the growth. Diamonds start out as a lump of coal and become what they are only after eons of intense heat and pressure. The strongest steels come from the hottest fires. Real gold does not fear the furnace, for it knows it is being purified. Oysters can produce beautiful pearls only after a tiny grain of sand irritates them for many years. An ugly caterpillar becomes a beautiful butterfly only when the time is right.

At the age of 70 I've seen it all, had a 30-year medical career and can speak from direct experience. Most of my life has been good but there have been some terrible happenings along the way . . . a failed marriage, family split, vicious custody battles, raising a teenage girl and boy, the suicide death

INTRODUCTION

of a younger brother, and struggles with the demons of an addiction to painkillers. I've also struggled with depression throughout my life.

One of my life's goals has been to write this book on optimism and positive thinking. My heroes in this field are many—Jesus Christ, Norman Vincent Peale, Dr. Robert Schuller, and Napoleon Hill (*Think and Grow Rich*). In American literature Mark Twain, Thomas Jefferson, and Johnny Appleseed stand out. In Chinese philosophy there are Confucius, Sun Tzu, and Lao Tzu. I have not gone too heavy on formal religion but do have a strong personal belief in God, Jesus Christ, guardian angels, and the afterlife. We are never alone in our struggles. Even if we cannot see, touch, smell, or hear these unseen powers, they are very much with us each and every day. All we have to do is ask for their help. Prayer is asking for their help, and meditation is waiting for an answer—often through intuitive insights. The premise of positive thinking is simple—whatever you can create and focus on in your mind you can create in physical reality. Anyone can do it. The Good News File is a technique I've used over the years in both my personal and professional life. When I was young, I began to see that good things do happen to us, often on a regular basis. Maybe it's an "attaboy" at work, or a much-feared situation turns out better than expected. When these good things happen we get a brief burst of dopamine in our brains, which goes away in 15 to 20 minutes. Then our brains drift back to the more painful problems in our lives—finances, health, legal and personal problems, which all demand our attention. We are all responsible for our mental, emotional, physical, and spiritual health. No matter how bad our problems are, we need to stay focused on the positive while dealing with our difficulties.

So when something good happens to me (or I have flashes of insight), I take a moment, write it down, and put it in my Good News File folder. Otherwise, I forget about it. Even when life is crashing down around me (and there's only one piece of good news), I write it down. It is always important to focus on what we have and not on what we don't. Then, every month or so when I'm feeling down, I take it out and read it. Within moments, I'm feeling better about myself and the world. The important thing is, you need *to write these things down.* Give it a try—it's cheaper than medications. After 50 years of doing this, my Good News File is over three feet thick.

It was also very helpful in my medical practice. If a patient was depressed, I'd say, "I can either put you on some antidepressant pills (many of which are helpful), or I can teach you to focus on the good things in your life." The majority of patients told me it worked and very few needed the pills. And the Good News File has been my main survival tool in dealing with the defeats and calamities that came my way. No matter how bad your life is now, there is always something good happening at the same time.

The human mind is a powerful thing. Whatever we focus or dwell upon becomes physical reality in the end. If we focus

INTRODUCTION

only on what's bad in our lives we eventually become neurotic and worry-filled people. If we stay focused on the good things, and daily show gratitude for what we have, our lives magically seem to improve themselves. This doesn't happen overnight, it takes time; but if we stick with it, it slowly but surely works in some special way.

Some "realists" criticize positive thinking as a way of life and thinking, claiming that it's an overly idealistic, platitude-filled way of life and ignoring the real problems in our lives. An "opiate for the masses," as some have said. There are so many problems out there in the world today and everyone's crying out that their own problems are the worst . . . the victim mentality. To listen to these folks we should all sit around every day and complain about our problems, as if that will somehow fix them. Yes, we all have a responsibility to face and deal with our problems in an effective manner, but why spend all our time on just the problems and not on the good things as well? While dealing with our problems, we can always stay upbeat by focusing on whatever good is happening to us at the same time, both past and present.

In 2005 (at the age of 55), I had a classic nervous breakdown after the breakdown of my marriage and family life, and hitting professional burnout in medicine. There followed the complete collapse of my mental, emotional, and physical lives, accompanied by a very bad addiction to painkillers. I lost everything—my medical and DEA licenses, my 30-year medical practice . . . basically my entire career in medicine.

THE GOOD NEWS FILE

I seriously contemplated suicide, but also knew it would have a devastating effect on my kids, my friends, and my family. We learned this horrible reality after the suicide death of my younger brother, Scott, who killed himself in 1992 at the age of 33. It hastened the deaths of both my parents (heartache is a very real thing). Suicide is a permanent solution to a temporary problem. No problem lasts forever. I wanted to see my kids grow up. My Good News File kept me going. It's taken me over 15 years to get my life back in order, largely with the help of both the Alcoholics and Narcotics Anonymous programs, as well as of a large group of supportive family and friends. I have since then regained both my sanity and my medical licenses. As Dr. Schuller's book says, "Tough times never last, but tough people do."

In the end, this is also what I've tried to teach my kids along the way. Hopefully these ideas can benefit you as well. These bits of wisdom have helped me and others lead happier and more productive lives, and deal with the toughest times that come our way. As I know your time is valuable, my writing is short, concise, and to the point. If you want a 600-page tome on the history of wisdom or a gripping novel, go elsewhere. Some writers like to expand and expound their ideas—I like to distill important ideas to their very essence, thus saving you time. You do not need to read this book at one sitting or from cover to cover. Just carry it with you each day and read a couple of thoughts at a time or whatever else interests you. And, if you feel it's helped, pass on whatever

INTRODUCTION

you learn to others. Like they say, pay it forward. In the end we will all have both good and bad experiences in our lives. It is just up to us to decide what we focus on.

Once again, the world needs hope. My goal in writing this book is to bring hope and inspiration to others. Every piece of wisdom in this book has helped and guided me at least once in my life. Hopefully these insights will help you as well. And don't let your high-tech, fast-paced lives cloud your concern for others—the people in your life are always the most important.

If I can inspire one person to lead a better and happier life, my mission is complete. Every day I find something to be happy about, and so can you.

Enjoy the book.

~ D. LYNN MICKLESON, MD
Palmer, Alaska
Summer 2020

The world needs all the help you can give by way of cheerful, optimistic, inspiring thought and personal example.

~ GRENVILLE KLEISER (1868–1953)
(American inspirational author)

2.0
WISDOM

2.1 Desiderata

Go placidly amid the noise and haste, and remember what peace there may be in silence. As far as possible without surrender be on good terms with all persons. Speak your truth quietly and clearly; and listen to others, even the dull and ignorant; they too have their story. Avoid loud and aggressive persons, they are vexatious to the spirit. If you compare yourself to others, you may become vain and bitter; for always there will be greater and lesser persons than yourself. Enjoy your achievements as well as your plans. Keep interested in your own career, however humble; it is a real possession in the changing fortunes of time. Exercise caution in your business affairs; for the world is full of trickery. But let this not blind you to what virtue there is; many persons strive for high ideals; and everywhere there is heroism. Be yourself. Especially do not feign affection. Neither be cynical about love; for in the face of all aridity and disenchantment it is as perennial as the grass. Take kindly the counsel of the years, gracefully surrendering the things of youth. Nurture strength of spirit to shield you in sudden misfortune. But do not distress yourself with imaginings. Many fears are born of fatigue and loneliness. Beyond a wholesome discipline, be gentle with yourself. You are a child of the universe, no less than the trees and the stars; you have a right to be here. And whether or not it is clear to you, no doubt the universe is unfolding as it should. Therefore be at peace with God, whatever you conceive Him to be; and whatever your labors and aspirations, in the noisy confusion of life, keep peace with your soul. With all its shams, drudgery, and broken dreams, it is still a beautiful world. Be careful. Strive to be happy.

~ Max Ehrmann
American Writer—1872–1945

2.2 Wisdom

Coincidences: There are no such things as coincidences. They are God's way of bringing the necessary people, events, and learning into our lives. If something new and unknown suddenly pops into your life, don't panic. Just wait awhile, and see how the situation becomes clearer to you. As the Chinese say, "Out of every crisis comes opportunity."

Always tell the truth: Never lie. If you always tell the truth, you never have to remember what you told other people.

Kindness should never be confused with weakness: It takes strength to practice kindness. If you want to win over enemies, just *kill them with kindness*. They'll be so surprised they'll probably end up being your friend. Kindness (and mercy) will win you many more friends than harshness. And, on being *nice*—remember that being too nice is as bad as not being nice at all—and people may wonder what your motives are, so always be sincere.

Respect: If you want respect, you must be willing to first give respect. Address senior men as *sir*, and senior women as *ma'am*. It may seem a bit old-fashioned, but it works. Love and respect the world, and the world will love and respect you. Also, it's nice to be liked but better to be respected. As Abe Lincoln once said, "You can please some of the people all of the time, and all of the people some of the time, but you can never please all of the people all of the time." It's better just to be yourself—people will recognize and respect you for being genuine. And remember, your actions will always speak louder than your words.

Still waters run deep: Many people make a lot of noise to gain attention, but quiet people often have a much greater depth. And, as the English poet John Dryden once said, "Beware the fury of a patient and quiet man."

Sticks and stones may break my bones, but words will never hurt ME: An old and maybe trite saying but very true. Believe in yourself and know that words are just that—words. People often say hurtful things when they themselves are hurting. Many people may be old in years, but just a scared little two-year-old child on the inside.

WISDOM

You can lead a horse to water but you cannot make it drink: In the same way, you may want to help a friend (and bring an opportunity to them), but unless they're ready (and want it), it won't do any good. So, always ask first if they even want your help. As the old saying goes, "The road to hell is paved with good intentions."

Sun Tzu's Art of War: A timeless work. Read and study this book's many lessons. It's not just about war—it can help you in many facets of your life.

Evil: Evil can be defined as someone making a conscious decision that ends up hurting other people. There are the *producers* in this world and there are the *thieves* who try to steal what the producers create and produce. On crime—99 times out of 100, crimes come down to love, hate, or money—and most common is money (or the fear of not having enough).

Also, never justify an action by saying "everyone else is doing it." This is a slippery road to evil and failure.

~ THE AUTHOR

Before judging someone, always walk a mile in their shoes.
~ OLD INDIAN SAYING

We are all personally responsible for the solutions to our problems and should never expect someone else to solve them. However, if help is needed, do your own best first, then don't be

afraid to ask for help. When family and friends come together to solve a problem, there is nothing that can stand in their way.
~ The Author

Full-moon craziness: Full-moon days and craziness are very real things. As an emergency room physician for many years, I saw this repeatedly. It starts about two days before until about a day after. Avoid making any major decisions or doing anything new or dangerous during this time. On full-moon days, just lock the front door, find a good book, and crawl in bed.
~ The Author

I'm not afraid of storms, for I am learning how to sail my ship.
~ Louisa May Alcott
(American novelist)

For someone with a hammer, everything starts looking like a nail.
~ Unknown

Talk is cheap: Always look at a person's actions to see what they're really about.
~ The Author

The greenest grass always grows over the septic tank . . . and the most beautiful lilies can grow over freshly dropped dung.
~ Unknown

WISDOM

(The lesson here is: Out of our worst situations can often grow beautiful things.)

True friends: True friends are there for you during the tough times. It's easy to say, "I love you," or "I'm your friend," but harder to prove with consistent action.

Hope for the best, prepare for the worst: If you see problems coming your way, do your best to prepare for them. As the military often says: "Hard in training, easy in war."
~ THE AUTHOR

The hard thing to do is often the right thing to do.
~ JOHN D. MACDONALD
(American author)

On buying things: If there's something you're thinking about buying, just ask yourself:
"Is this a *need* . . . or is it a *want*?"
~ THE AUTHOR

You can never plan the future by the past.
~ EDMUND BURKE (1729–1797)
(Irish statesman)

(Yes, it's always necessary to study history, so that you learn from the mistakes of the past, but new thinking is always needed for new problems.)

2.3 The Station

Tucked away in our subconscious is an idyllic vision. We see ourselves on a long trip that spans the continent. We are traveling by train. Out the windows we drink in the passing scene of cars on nearby highways.

But uppermost in our minds is the final destination. On a certain day at a certain hour we will put into the station. Bands will be playing and flags waving. Once we get there many wonderful dreams will come true and the pieces of our lives will fit together like a completed jigsaw puzzle. How restlessly we pace the aisles, damning the minutes for loitering—waiting, waiting, waiting for the station.

"When we reach the station, that will be it!" we cry.
"When I'm 18."
"When I buy a new 450 SL Mercedes Benz."
"When I put my last kid through college."

WISDOM

"When I have paid off the mortgage."
"When I get a promotion."
"When I reach the age of retirement,
I shall live happily ever after!"

Sooner or later we must realize there is no station, no one place to arrive at once and for all. The true joy of life is the trip. The station is only a dream. It constantly outdistances us.

So, stop pacing the aisles and counting the miles. Instead, climb more mountains, eat more ice cream, go barefoot more often, swim more rivers, watch more sunsets, laugh more, cry less. Life must be lived as we go along.

The station will come soon enough.

~ ROBERT J. HASTINGS
(American inspirational author)

2.4 Law of Unintended Consequences

Once upon a time in the old West there was a rancher with a corral full of fine horses. One day his prize stallion jumped the fence and ran away, breaking the fence in the process. His neighbors came over and said, "Oh, that's horrible news!" but the rancher just said, "It ain't good news, and it ain't bad news, it just is."

Several days later his stallion returned—leading a group of beautiful wild mares. Again his neighbors came over, this time saying, "That's wonderful news." The rancher again said, "Well, it ain't good news and it ain't bad news, it just is."

A week later his son attempted to ride and break the fine stallion. In the process, he fell off and broke his leg. The neighbors came again and said, "Oh, that's horrible news!" But the rancher just said, "It ain't good news and it ain't bad news, it just is." Exasperated, the neighbors just walked away.

WISDOM

A month later an army recruiter came calling (as the war was on). He took one look at the injured son and said, "Well, son, I'm sorry but I can't take you because of your broken leg," and walked away. The neighbors came over and said, "Oh, that's great news, your son doesn't need to go to war!" And the rancher said once again: "It ain't good news and it ain't bad news, it just is."

Moral of the Story

If calamity or catastrophe strikes, don't rush to judge the consequences—don't panic, be patient, and wait until the dust settles before you do anything. It is often said that for something new to be born, something old must first die. Where one door closes, another one always opens.

~ **Source unknown**

2.5 The Seeds of Character

Ling was thrilled. He had been invited—along with all the young people throughout the land—to a special assembly with the emperor.

When Ling arrived at the gates of the palace, he was given a seed and escorted to the Great Hall. Other children were already gathered there, and after a short while, the emperor came before them and spoke, "The successor to my throne stands among you in the crowd today. Each person here has been given a seed. This seed will determine your future. You are to plant it, water it every day, and return here in one year with the fruits of your labor."

Ling rushed home and planted his seed in a pot of soil. Did he really have a chance to be the next ruler? He watered the soil and placed the pot in a window where it would get the most sun.

Days passed and nothing grew. So Ling fertilized the soil, yet nothing grew. Months went by and his pot stood barren.

WISDOM

Finally, the day arrived when the young people were to return to the palace. Ling was so ashamed of his failure that he decided not to go. But his mother said, "Ling, you have nothing to be ashamed of. You have done what was asked of you. Return to the palace and be honest about your results."

Ling knew his mother was right. But when he arrived at the palace, he saw an abundance of plants—some with dazzling flowers, others with canopies of foliage. Ling became embarrassed by his efforts. He picked a spot at the back of the crowd, hoping to conceal his failure.

The emperor swept into the room and surveyed the plants. Ling held his breath as the emperor spotted him. "You, in the corner there. Come forward."

Ling reluctantly approached the emperor. The other kids began to snicker as he passed by with his pot of soil. "What is your name?" asked the emperor.

"I am Ling, Your Majesty."

The emperor bowed to Ling, saying, "One year ago I gave each of you a boiled seed that could not grow. Yet, today I see every kind of plant that grows in our land! Ling is the only one among you with enough honesty to bring back an empty pot and face possible ridicule and reproach. That kind of integrity shows nobility. All bow to your next ruler, Ling!"

~ Adapted from the Afterhours
Inspirational Stories Website

2.6 A Quiz

The following is something to make us stop and think...

1. Name the five wealthiest people in the world.
2. Name the last five Heisman trophy winners.
3. Name the last five winners of the Miss America contest.
4. Name ten people who have won the Nobel or Pulitzer Prize.
5. Name the last half dozen Academy Award winners for best actor and actress.
6. Name the last decade's worth of World Series winners.

How did you do?

The point is—none of us remember the headliners of yesterday. These are no second-rate achievers. They are the

WISDOM

best in their fields. But the applause dies. Awards tarnish. Achievements are forgotten. Accolades and certifications are buried with their owners.

Here's another quiz. See how you do on this one:

1. List a few teachers who aided your journey through school.
2. Name three friends who have helped you through a difficult time.
3. Name five people who have taught you something worthwhile.
4. Think of five people you enjoy spending time with.
5. Think of a few people who have made you feel appreciated and special.
6. Name half a dozen heroes whose stories have inspired you.

Easier? The lesson? The people who have made a difference in your life are not the ones with the most credentials, the most money, or the most awards. They are the ones who care. You will always be remembered for the kindnesses you show and not for how smart you are. Pass this on to those people who have made a difference in your life.

~ UNKNOWN

2.7 Some Thoughts for a Vital Life

Play by the rules.
Honesty isn't the best policy—it's the only policy.
Admit when you're wrong.
Do the right thing—do things right.
Don't settle for anything less than the very best.
Love flag and country.
Show respect for others.
Maintain impeccable integrity.
Don't be bullheaded.
Always be on time—even early.
Revere your heritage and roots.
Listen before you speak. Listen. Listen!
Take the cotton out of your ears and put it in your mouth.

(FROM AA)

WISDOM

Be childlike, not childish.
Courtesy is contagious—start an epidemic.
Keep your word.
Show appreciation often and spontaneously.
You don't have a second chance to make a first impression.
You can do it!
Love your God with all your heart.
The word *you* is more important than *me* or *I*.
Take time to enjoy life.
Apologize, and mean it.
Don't get angry—maybe the other person is having a bad day.
What goes around comes around.
Practice humility.

~ UNKNOWN

2.8 Laws of Life

Even if don't believe in them, these laws of life will still apply to me, just like the law of gravity does. If I don't believe in gravity, the splat I make won't be any smaller than if I do believe in it.

On my journey through life, things are not always fair, so if I wait for things to be fair before I get moving, it's going to be a slooooow trip.

I can't always choose what happens to me, but I can choose how I react to what happens.

Although there may be reasons why some things are harder for me, it won't help to use them as excuses.

Sooner or later, I will have more freedom by following rules and laws than by breaking them.

I never have the right to give up trying, unless I want to choose failure.

WISDOM

I have to honestly love and appreciate me before I can really love and appreciate anyone else.

If I choose a fight-or-flight response to a problem, the problem will still be there the next day.

~ STANTON STARR (AMERICAN WRITER)

2.9 The Four Agreements

Be Impeccable with Your Word
Speak with integrity. Say only what you mean. Avoid using the word to speak against yourself or to gossip about others. Use the power of your word in the direction of truth and love.

Don't take anything personally
Nothing others do is because of you. What others say and do is a projection of their own reality, their own dream. When you are immune to the opinions and actions of others, you won't be the victim of needless suffering.

Don't make assumptions
Find the courage to ask questions and to express what you really want. Communicate with others as clearly as you can to avoid misunderstandings, sadness, and drama. With just this one agreement, you can completely transform your life.

WISDOM

Always do your best

Your best is going to change from moment to moment. It will be different when you are healthy as opposed to when you are sick. Under any circumstances, simply do your best and you will avoid self-judgment, self-abuse, and regret.

~ Don Miguel Ruiz

(From the Toltec religion, precursors of the Aztecs)

2.10 An Ethical Will

1. Be honest.
2. Be a person whom others are justified in trusting.
3. If you say you will do something, do it.
4. You don't have to be the best, but you should be the best you can be.
5. Treat all people with respect and courtesy—no exceptions.
6. Remember the way to be happy is to think of what you can do for others. The way to be miserable is to think about what people should be doing for you.
7. Be part of something bigger than your own self. That something can be family, pursuit of knowledge, the environment, or whatever you choose.
8. Remember that hard work is satisfying and fulfilling.
9. Nurture the ability to laugh and have fun.

WISDOM

10. Have a respect for those who have gone before; learn from their mistakes and weaknesses; build on their strengths.

~ Frank Perdue (1920–2005)
(Founder, Perdue Farms)

2.11 Instructions for Life

1. Take into account that great love and great achievement involve great risk.
2. When you lose love, don't lose the lessons.
3. Follow the three *R*s: Respect for self. Respect for others. Responsibility for all your actions.
4. Remember that not getting what you want is sometimes a wonderful stroke of luck.
5. Learn the rules so you know how to avoid difficulties.
6. Don't let a little dispute injure a great friendship.
7. When you realize you've made a mistake, take immediate steps to correct it.
8. Spend some time alone every day.
9. Open your arms to change, but don't let go of your values.
10. Corollary—it's good to be open-minded, but not so open your brains fall out.

WISDOM

11. Remember that silence is sometimes the best answer.
12. Live a good, honorable life. Then, when you get older and think back, you'll be able to enjoy it a second time.
13. In disagreements with loved ones, deal only with the current situation. Don't bring up the past.
14. Share your knowledge. It's a way to achieve immortality.
15. Be gentle with the earth.
16. Once a year, go someplace you've never been before.
17. Remember that the best relationship is one in which your love for each other exceeds your need for each other.
18. Judge your success by what you had to give up in order to get it.
19. Approach love and cooking with reckless abandon.

~ THE DALAI LAMA

(Tibetan spiritual leader)

2.12 Dealing with the Burdens of Life

1. Always keep your words soft and sweet, just in case you need to eat them.
2. Drive carefully. It's not only cars that can be recalled by their maker.
3. If you can't be kind, at least have the decency to be vague.
4. If you lend someone twenty dollars and never see that person again, it was probably worth it.
5. It may be that your sole purpose in life is simply to be kind to others.
6. Never put both feet in your mouth at the same time, because then you won't have a leg to stand on.
7. Nobody cares if you can't dance well. Just get up and dance.
8. The second mouse gets the cheese.

WISDOM

9. When everything's coming your way, you're probably in the wrong lane.
10. You may be only one person in the world, but you may also be the world to one person.
11. We could learn a lot from crayons—some are sharp, some are pretty, and some are dull. Some have weird names, and all are different colors, but they all have to live in the same box.
12. A truly happy person is one who can enjoy the scenery on a detour.
13. Accept that some days you're the pigeon, and some days you're the statue.

Have an awesome day and know that someone has thought about you today . . . I did.

~ UNKNOWN

2.13 How Do You Live Your Dash?

I read of a man who stood to speak
At the funeral of a friend.
He referred to the dates on the tombstone
From the beginning . . . to the end.

He noted that first came her date of birth
And spoke the following date with tears,
But he said what mattered most of all
Was the dash between those years . . . 1934–1998.

For that dash represents all the time
That she spent alive on earth . . .
And now only those who loved her,
Know what that little line is worth.

WISDOM

For it matters not, how much we own;
The cars, the house, the cash,
What matter most is how we live and love
And how we spend our dash.

So think about this long and hard—
Are there things you'd like to change?
For you never know how much time is left,
That can still be rearranged.

If we could just slow down enough
To consider what's true and real,
And always try to understand
The way other people feel.

And be less quick to anger,
And show appreciation more,
And love the people in our lives,
Like we've never loved before.

If we treat each other with respect,
And more often wear a smile . . .
Remembering that this special dash
Might only last a little while.

THE GOOD NEWS FILE

So, when your eulogy's being read
With your life's actions to rehash—
Would you be proud of the things they say
About how you spent your dash?

And what will your own tombstone read?

~ Unknown

2.14 A Blueprint for Living

To stand tall in the sunlight
To seek out the bright face of beauty
To search for the dream, the star
To see the world through eyes of tenderness
To love with openheartedness
To speak the quiet word of comforting
To look up to the mountain and not be afraid to climb
To be aware of the needs of others
To believe in the wonder of life,
The miracle of creation,
The rapture of love,
The beauty of the universe,
The dignity of the human being.

~ KATHERINE NELSON DAVIS
(Australian author)

2.15 Lao Tzu

A great nation is like a great man—when he makes a mistake, he realizes it. Having realized it, he admits it. Having admitted it, he corrects it. He considers those who point out his faults as his most benevolent teachers. He thinks of his enemy as the shadow that he himself casts.

If a nation is centered in the Tao, if it nourishes its own people and doesn't meddle in the affairs of others, it will be a light to all nations of the world.

All streams flow to the sea because it is lower than they are. Humility gives it its power.

If you want to govern the people, you must place yourself below them. If you want to lead the people, you must learn how to follow them.

WISDOM

Governing a large country is like frying a small fish. You spoil it with too much poking.

Center your country in the Tao and evil will have no power. Not that it isn't there, but you'll be able to step out of its way.

Give evil nothing to oppose and it will disappear by itself.

The greater the number of laws and enactments, the more thieves and robbers there will be.

To the individualist, government, with its laws and regulations more numerous than the hairs of an ox, was a vicious oppressor of the individual, and more to be feared than fierce tigers.

Government, in sum, must be limited to the smallest possible minimum; inaction is the proper function of government, since only inaction can permit the individual to flourish and achieve happiness.

Any intervention by government, Lao-Tzu declared, would be counterproductive, and would lead to confusion and turmoil.

After referring to the common experience of mankind with government, Lao Tzu came to this incisive conclusion: The more artificial taboos and restrictions there are in the world, the more people are impoverished.

If I keep from meddling with people, they take care of themselves.

If I keep from commanding people, they behave themselves.

If I keep from preaching at people, they improve themselves.

If I keep from imposing on people, they become themselves.

"A leader," the wise man goes on, "is best when people barely know he exists; when his work is done, his aim fulfilled, they will say we did it ourselves."

Stop trying to control.

Let go of fixed plans and concepts, and the world will govern itself.

The more prohibitions you have, the less virtuous people will be. The more weapons you have, the less secure people will be. The more subsidies you have, the less self-reliant people will be.

When taxes are too high, people go hungry. When government is too intrusive, people lose their spirit.

Act for the people's benefit. Trust them, leave them alone. If you don't trust the people, you make them untrustworthy.

"Therefore," the Master says, "I let go of the law, and people become honest. I let go of economics, and people become prosperous. I let go of religion, and people become serene. I let go of all desire for common good and the good becomes as common as grass."

Without laws or compulsion, men would dwell in harmony.

WISDOM

The wisest course, then, is to keep the government simple and for it to take no action, for then the world stabilizes itself.

As Lao-Tzu put it, "Therefore I take no action, yet the people transform themselves, I favor quiescence and the people right themselves, I take no action, and the people enrich themselves."

~ Lao-Tzu
Chinese philosopher
(6th–5th century BC)

2.16 Abraham Lincoln

If you sometimes get discouraged, consider this fellow:

He dropped out of grade school.
Ran a country store.
Went broke.
Took 15 years to pay off his bills.
Took a wife.
Unhappy marriage.
Ran for House.
Lost twice.
Ran for Senate.
Lost twice.
Delivered speech that became a classic.
Audience indifferent.
Suffered recurrent episodes of severe, suicidal depression.

WISDOM

Attacked daily by the press and despised by half the country. Despite all this, imagine how many people all over the world have been inspired by this awkward, rumpled, brooding man who signed his name simply, A. Lincoln

When I do good, I feel good. That's my religion.

No man has a good enough memory to be a good liar.

Most folks are as happy as they make up their minds to be.

*The best thing about the future is that
it comes one day at a time.*

*Give me six hours to chop down a tree, and I will
spend the first four sharpening the axe.*

*You cannot escape the responsibility of
tomorrow by evading it today.*

I am not bound to win, but I am bound to be true.

*I am not bound to succeed, but I am bound
to live by the light that I have.*

*I must stand with anybody that stands right, and stand with
him while he is right, and part with him when he goes wrong.*

THE GOOD NEWS FILE

Sir, my concern is not whether God is on our side;
my greatest concern is to be on God's side,
for God is always right.

I do the very best I know how, the very best I can;
and I mean to keep on doing so until the end.

I don't like that man.
I must get to know him better.

Be sure to put your feet in the right place,
then stand firm.

The philosophy of the school room in one generation
will be the philosophy of government in the next.

We the people are the rightful masters of both Congress
and the courts, not to overthrow the Constitution,
but to overthrow the men who pervert the Constitution.

My great concern is not whether you have failed,
but whether you are content with your failure.

It has been my experience that folks who
have no vices have very few virtues.

I am a slow walker but I never walk back.

WISDOM

I will prepare and someday my chance will come.

The dogmas of the quiet past are inadequate to the stormy present. The occasion is piled high with difficulty, and we must rise with the occasion. As our case is new, so we must think anew and act anew.

I have always found that mercy bears richer fruits than strict justice.

Don't worry when you are not recognized, but strive to be worthy of recognition.

Do I not destroy my enemies when I make them my friends?

Always bear in mind that your own resolution to succeed is more important than any other.

Don't interfere with anything in the Constitution. That must be maintained, for it is the only safeguard of our liberties.

Towering genius disdains a beaten path. It seeks regions hitherto unexplored.

I like to see a man proud of the place in which he lives. I like to see a man live so that his place will be proud of him.

THE GOOD NEWS FILE

I do not think much of a man who is not wiser today than he was yesterday.

There is no grievance that is a fit object of redress by mob law.

I never had a policy; I just try to do my best each and every day.

The shepherd drives the wolf from the sheep's throat, for which the sheep thanks the shepherd as his liberator, while the wolf denounces him as the destroyer of liberty. Plainly, the sheep and the wolf are not agreed upon a definition of liberty.

We should be too big to take offense and too noble to give it.

What kills a skunk is the publicity it gives itself.

The ballot is stronger than the bullet.

Let's have faith that right makes might; and in that faith let us, to the end, dare to do our duty as we understand it.

~ ABRAHAM LINCOLN (1809–1865)
(16th U.S. President)

2.17 A Zen Story

Once upon a time two Zen masters came to a pond.
They wanted to cross it.
A *lady of the night* is also there.
She wants to cross it.
The older Zen master says,
"Hey, I will carry you on my back."
The lady hops onto his back.
All three wade across the pond.
At the other side of the pond the older Zen
master puts her down and she goes on her way.
The younger Zen monk is *shocked*.
SHOCKED! Isn't it a sin to carry around
a woman like that?
He keeps thinking about it and thinking about it
while they silently go down the road.
Finally, an hour or so later, he speaks up.

THE GOOD NEWS FILE

"It's against everything we stand for."
The older Zen master looks at him for a moment
and says, "I put her down hours ago.
Why are you still carrying her?"

~ OLD ZEN BUDDHIST STORY

2.18 Civilization

Civilization is like a stream with banks.
The stream is sometimes filled with people stealing,
shouting and doing the things historians usually record,
while on the banks, unnoticed, people build homes,
make love, raise children, sing songs, write poetry,
and even whittle statues.
The story of civilization is the story of what
happened on the banks.
Historians are pessimists because they ignore
the banks for the river.

~ WILL DURANT (1885–1981)
(American Historian)

2.19 Why Is There Hatred?

The history of the world can often be explained as the eternal conflict between the *haves* and *have-nots*. In physics, cold always drains heat. There are many similarities in the human world. Look at the differences between people and you can often understand their behavior:

Poor people envy rich people.

Short people envy tall people.

Obese people envy slim people.

Unattractive people envy attractive people.

Minorities envy majorities.

WISDOM

Outgroups envy ingroups.

Losers envy winners.

Sad people envy happy people.

Sick people envy healthy people.

Unpopular people envy popular people.

Weak people envy strong people.

Etc., etc., etc.

~ **The Author**

2.20 On Slavery

Slavery has existed in the world for thousands of years.
Blacks were not enslaved because they were Black,
but because they were available.
African tribal chiefs sold their prisoners of war
to white slave traders.
Whites enslaved other Whites in Europe
for centuries before the first Black was brought
to the Western hemisphere.
Asians enslaved Europeans.
Asians enslaved other Asians.
Africans enslaved other Africans,
and, indeed, even today in North Africa,
Blacks continue to enslave other Blacks.

~ THOMAS SOWELL (1930—PRESENT)
(Black historian)

2.21 Benjamin Franklin

I made it a rule to forbear all direct contradiction to the sentiment of others, and all positive assertions of my own. I ever forbade myself the use of every word or expression in the language that imported a fix'd opinion . . . for these 50 years past no one has ever heard a dogmatical expression escape me.

Tact is the art of making a point without making an enemy.

> Who is wise? He that learns from every One.
> Who is powerful? He that governs his Passions.
> Who is rich? He that is Content.
> Who is that? Nobody.

> To whom thy secret thou dost tell,
> To him thy freedom thou dost sell.

THE GOOD NEWS FILE

Be civil to all; serviceable to many;
Familiar with few;
Friend to one; Enemy to no one.

He that would live in peace and at ease,
Must not speak all he knows,
Nor judge all he sees.

If you would not be forgotten,
As soon as you are dead and rotten,
Either write things worth reading,
Or do things worth the writing.

~ **BENJAMIN FRANKLIN**
(From *Poor Richard's Almanac*)

Franklin's Epitaph

The Body of
B. Franklin, Printer
(Like the Cover of an old Book
Its contents worn out,
And stript of Its Lettering and Gilding)
Lies here, Food for Worms.
But the work shall not be lost,
For it will (as he believ'd) appear once more,

WISDOM

In a new and more elegant edition
Revised and corrected.

~ By the Author
(Our loving God)

~ Benjamin Franklin (1706–1790)
(American statesman)

2.22 Education

Whom, then, do I call educated?
First, those who control circumstances
instead of being mastered by them,
those who meet all occasions manfully,
and act in accordance with intelligent
thinking, those who are honorable in all
dealings, who treat good-naturedly
persons and things that are disagreeable;
and furthermore, those who hold their
pleasures under control and are not
overcome by misfortune; finally, those
who are not spoiled by success.

~ Socrates (470–399 BC)
(Greek scholar)

WISDOM

Education is an admirable thing,
but it is well to remember from time to time
that nothing that is worth knowing
can be taught in a school. Life's experiences
are always the best teacher.

~ KATHARINE HEPBURN (FROM OSCAR WILDE)
(American actress)

3.0
SPIRITUAL WELLNESS

3.1 Talk to the Potter

There was a couple who took a trip to England to shop in a beautiful antique store to celebrate their twenty-fifth wedding anniversary. They both liked teacups. Spotting an exceptional cup, they said to the proprietor: "May we see that? We've never seen a cup quite so beautiful."

As the lady handed it to them, suddenly the teacup spoke, "You don't understand. I have not always been a teacup; there was a time when I was just a lump of red clay. My master took me and rolled me, pounded and patted me, over and over and I yelled out, 'I don't like it! Leave me alone,' but he only smiled and gently said 'Not yet!'

"Then WHAM! I was placed on a spinning wheel and went around and around and around. 'Stop it! I'm getting so dizzy! I'm going to be sick!' I screamed. But the master only nodded and said quietly, 'Not yet.'

"He spun me and poked and prodded and bent me out of shape and then he put me in the oven. I never felt such heat. I yelled and knocked and pounded at the door. 'Help! Get me out of here!' 'Not yet,' he said.

"When I thought I couldn't bear it another minute, the door opened. He carefully took me out and put me on the shelf, and I began to cool.

"Then suddenly he put me back into the oven. This one was twice as hot and I just knew I would suffocate—but I didn't. As he took me out, I thought, 'What's he going to do to me next!'

"An hour later he handed me a mirror and said, 'Look.' And I did. I said, 'That's not me; that couldn't be me. It's beautiful. I'm beautiful!'

"Quietly he spoke: 'I know it hurt to be rolled and pounded, but had I just left you alone, you'd have dried up. I know it was hot and disagreeable in the oven, but if I hadn't put you there, you would have cracked. I know the fumes were bad when I brushed and painted you all over, but if I hadn't done that, you never would have hardened. You would not have had any color in your life. If I hadn't put you in that second oven, you wouldn't have survived for long because the hardness would not have held. Now you are a finished product. Now you are what I had in mind when I first began with you.'"

The moral of this story is this: God knows what He's doing for each of us. He is the potter and we are His clay. He will

SPIRITUAL WELLNESS

mold us and make us and expose us to just enough pressures of just the right kinds that we may be made into a flawless piece of work to fulfill His good, pleasing, and perfect will.

So, when life seems hard, and you are being pounded and patted and pushed almost beyond endurance; when your world seems to be spinning out of control; when you feel like you are in a fiery furnace of trials, when life seems to *stink* (a.k.a. *is crappy*): Try this—brew a cup of your favorite tea (or coffee) in your prettiest cup, sit down, and then have a little talk with the Potter.

~ Patricia Kimerer
(*Tribune Chronicle* Newspaper)

3.2 Spirituality

Faith: Faith is the belief in things unseen. Put the problem in God's hands and He will guide you to the right decision. Master faith and you will automatically master fear.

Works in progress: We are all *works in progress*. Be easy and kind on yourself as you deal with life's struggles. Nobody's perfect, and all you can do is the best with whatever you've got each and every day. If someone angers or hurts you, don't take it personally. Maybe that person is having a bad day, is in pain, or overwhelmed by their own problems and just wants to lash out at someone.

What would Jesus do: *WWJD* was a famous phrase in the 1990s. There is great wisdom in this, so whenever you're uncertain about what do in a situation, just follow *WWJD*— and also just be yourself.

SPIRITUAL WELLNESS

Challenges: Regardless of whatever challenge you are facing now, know that it has not come to stay. It will pass eventually. During these times, do what you can with what you have, and ask for help if needed. Most important, never surrender. Put things in perspective. Take care of yourself and stay healthy. Find ways to replenish your energy, strengthen your faith, and fortify yourself from the inside out.

~ Caring Bridge
(Cancer support group)

Reincarnation: Reincarnation does exist. It is impossible for each of us to learn all the necessary lessons about life in just one lifetime. Think of your physical body as a rental car at an airport. We fly in, pick up the car, drive it for 75 years, return it to the airport, then fly away for another cycle of life. You will be given one physical body life for this lifetime, so take good care of it. Think of each lifetime as a grade in school from kindergarten to twelfth grade. In each life/grade, we progress in knowledge and the ability to love others until we finally reach perfection—as in the life and personality of Jesus Christ. He represented the ideal combination of male and female virtues. Mind, Energy, and Will of the male . . . and Love, Nurturing, and Wisdom of the female.

~ The Author

THE GOOD NEWS FILE

Unhappiness: *The source of all unhappiness is failed expectations.*

~ Gautama Buddha

Are you expecting too much from other people? If you are, just begin by looking at yourself first. Are *you* perfect? If not, then you cannot expect perfection from others. Be reasonable in your expectations and demands of others, and you will lead a much happier life. Be aware also that *other people's behavior is often a reflection of our own.* Be positive and others will respond in kind. Be negative and negativity will follow. And remember this, if you cannot love yourself, you cannot love anyone else at all, so be sure to love yourself first and foremost.

Forgiveness: Forgiveness mainly helps you, not the offending party. You may never forget what someone has done to you, but you *can* release your anger toward them. Anger, hate, and resentments are heavy burdens and will corrode your soul . . . and weaken you in the end. Do your best to resolve resentments. Pray for your enemies—hard to do, but effective.

Worry: Worry is a waste of time and energy. The things we worry most about usually do not come true. In my own life, 90 percent of the things I ever worried about never came to pass . . . and the other 10 percent weren't as bad as I feared. Yes, there are occasional random disasters beyond our control, but just stay cool, and don't panic. So, yes, it's OK to be concerned about the problems in our lives, but just do your best each day with whatever you've got, and get a good night's sleep.

~ The Author

Cycles: Our lives always go in cycles—good times and bad times, happy times and dark times, periods of hell and periods of heaven, but just as day follows night, the bad times never last. Occasional bad experiences are necessary so we can better identify and appreciate the good times when they finally come.

Karma: Karma is real—what goes around comes around. Whatever good and kindness you put out in the world spreads like ripples in a pond. Same with bad deeds. And, like ripples in a pond, they hit the edge and bounce back toward the center. Your kindnesses (and bad deeds as well) will always come back to you manifold. Just be patient. Be aware also that these karmic effects may not return to you in this lifetime, but will surely follow you in future ones.

Revenge: *Living well is the best revenge* is an important concept. There's an old Chinese saying: "If you're going to seek revenge, always dig two holes, and bring two caskets—one for your enemy, and one for yourself." In the Old Testament, it says, "An eye for an eye, and a tooth for a tooth," but what does this accomplish? It only ends up with two blind and toothless people. Remember also what Francis Bacon (English statesman, 1561–1626) once said, "In taking revenge, a man is but even with his enemy; but in passing it over, he is superior."

All's well that ends well: We all go through storms in our lives and it often seems we'll fall apart in the process. If we're alive and standing at the end, consider it another learning lesson in life. As the Germans say, "What does not kill me, makes me stronger." Remember that God never gives us more than we can handle. Pain, whether it's mental, emotional, physical, or spiritual tells us something is wrong and motivates us to find the source of the pain and get rid of it. Even if we fail at solving that pain or problem, even if we make mistakes along the way, it shows that we are at least trying. It all works out in the end—just as it should. And, as Dr. Robert Schuller has often said, "Tough times never last, but tough people do."

Truth and beauty: For all the problems in the world, there is still a lot of truth and beauty out there. Always look for it. If you constantly focus on the good, happiness will soon follow. Yes, we all have problems; just do your daily best to deal with them, but keep your focus on the good things. As Alaric Hutchinson, the famous interfaith minister, once said, "Find something beautiful to focus on each day, then allow inspiration to have its way with you."

SPIRITUAL WELLNESS

Positive thinking: Always surround yourself with positive and helpful people. Seek out those who can help you with your own spiritual development.

Sleeping on a problem: is often a great way to solve a problem. Let your subconscious mind work on it overnight, and you'll be surprised what answers come to you in the morning. And, as the Irish say, "A good laugh and a long sleep are the two best cures for anything."

Flow of life: If you seem to be carried along in something bigger than yourself, don't fight it—just go with the flow. Stay flexible, and adapt to whatever changes come along.

Theft: If someone steals something from you, maybe that person needs it more than you do.

> *To thine own self be true.*
> ~ **WILLIAM SHAKESPEARE (1564–1616)**
> (English playwright)

> ***Soul development:*** *When the student is ready, the teacher will appear.*
> ~ **BUDDHIST SAYING**

> *Just keep learning, be patient, and your teacher will show up at the right time.*

THE GOOD NEWS FILE

A moral act is something you feel good after.
~ Ernest Hemingway
(American novelist)

When a human being never takes any emotional risks,
they never get hurt—but then again, they're never alive.
~ John D. MacDonald
(American author)

3.3 Ascension

And if I go,
while you're still here . . .
Know that I live on,
vibrating to a different measure
—behind a thin veil you cannot see through.
You will not see me,
so you must have faith.
I wait for the time when we can soar together again,
—both aware of each other.
Until then, live your life to the fullest,
And when you need me,
Just whisper my name in your heart,
. . . I will be there.

~ Dr. Colleen Corah Hitchcock
(Clinical hypnotist)

3.4 Helping Others

Everybody can be great . . .
because everybody can serve.
You don't have to have a college degree to serve.
You don't have to make your subject and verb agree to serve.
You don't have to know about Plato and Aristotle to serve.
You don't have to know Einstein's Theory of
Relativity to serve.
You don't have to know the second theory of
thermodynamics in physics to serve.
You only need a heart full of grace and
a soul generated by love.
You don't have to see the whole staircase,
just take the first step.

~ Rev. Martin Luther King Jr
(Civil rights leader)

3.5 Law of the Garbage Truck

One day I hopped in a taxi and we took off for the airport. We were driving in the right lane when suddenly a black car jumped out of a parking space right in front of us. My taxi driver slammed on his brakes, skidded, and missed the other car by just inches!

The driver of the other car whipped his head around and started yelling at us. My taxi driver just smiled and waved at the guy. And I mean, he was really friendly.

So I asked, "Why did you just do that? The guy almost ruined your car and sent us to the hospital!"

This is when my taxi driver taught me what I now call, *The Law of the Garbage Truck*.

He explained that many people are like garbage trucks. They run round full of garbage, full of frustration, full of anger, and full of disappointment. As their garbage piles up, they need a place to dump it, and sometimes they'll dump it on you. Don't take it personally. Just smile, wave, wish them well, and move on. Don't take their garbage and spread it to other people at work, at home, or on the streets.

The bottom line is that successful people do not let garbage trucks take over their day. Life's too short to wake up in the morning with regrets, so love the people who treat you right. Pray for the ones who don't.

Life is 10 percent what you make it and 90 percent how you take it!

Have a blessed, garbage-free day.

~ UNKNOWN

3.6 The Law

Your path may be clouded—uncertain your goal,
Move on, for the orbit is fixed for your soul,

And though it may lead into the darkness of night,
The torch of the builder shall give it new light.

You were—and you will be—know this while you are,
Your spirit has traveled both long and afar.

It came from a source and to a source it returns,
The spark that was lighted eternally burns.

From body to body your spirit speeds on—
It seeks a new form when the old one is gone.

THE GOOD NEWS FILE

And the form that it finds is the fabric you wrought
On the loom of the mind, with the fiber of thought.

Somewhere on some planet—sometime and somehow
Your life will reflect all the thoughts of you now.

The Law is unerring—no blood can atone,
The structure you rear—you live in it alone.

As dew is drawn upward, in rain to descend,
Your thoughts drift away and in destiny blend.

You cannot escape them, for petty or great,
Or evil or noble—they fashion your fate.

From cycle to cycle—through time and through space
Your lives with your longing will ever keep pace.

And all that you ask for—and all you desire;
Must come to your longing—as flames out of fire.

~ **Ella Wheeler Wilcox**
(American author/poet)

3.7 The Privilege of Life

While you have the privilege of life on this earth—and it is a privilege, in spite of unceasing problems—you should live. You should live, whether you are 16 or 65.

Be like Enzio Pinza, an inspiration to millions when he starred in *South Pacific*, reaching his age when others allow themselves to decay; he was far younger in spirit than some less fortunate people in their early twenties.

Naturally, older age requires a person to place sensible limits on their physical capabilities. When you are older, you can't run around like a young kid, and if you have a heart condition, you must further restrict your activities. Yet the older person has qualities that the child or adolescent hasn't even begun to develop.

The main point is, in older age, each day can be thrilling. It's up to you. Even if you are over 65 and have already wasted time moping—stop blaming yourself. You're not perfect, no one is, and self-blame will not help you. You must have self-respect as long as you live—so live creatively every day of your life.

When Pablo Casals reached 95, a young reporter threw him a question: "Mr. Casals, you are 95 and the greatest cellist who ever lived. Why do you still practice six hours a day?"

And Mr. Casals answered, "Because I think I'm making progress."

Your goal is to make progress every day of your life.

~ Dr. Maxwell Maltz
(American surgeon and author of *Psycho-Cybernetics*)

3.8 Love—The One Creative Force

Spread love wherever you go;
First of all in your own house.
Give love to your children,
to your wife or husband,
to a next-door neighbor . . .
Let no one ever come to you
without leaving better and happier.
Be the living expression of God's kindness;
kindness in your face,
kindness in your eyes,
kindness in your smile,
kindness in your warm greeting.

~ MOTHER TERESA
(Indian saint)

THE GOOD NEWS FILE

If there is light in the soul,
There will be beauty in the person.
If there is beauty in the person,
There will be harmony in the house.
If there is harmony in the house,
There will be order in the nation.
If there is order in the nation,
There will be peace in the world.

~ **Chinese proverb**

3.9 A Creed for Those Who Have Suffered

I asked God for strength, that I might achieve—
I was made weak, that I might learn humbly to obey.

I asked for health, that I might do great things—
I was given infirmity, that I might do better things.

I asked for riches, that I might be happy—
I was given poverty, that I might be wise.

I asked for power, that I might have the praise of men—
I was given weakness, that I might feel the need of God.

I asked for all things, that I might enjoy life—
I was given life, that I might enjoy all things.

THE GOOD NEWS FILE

I got nothing I asked for—
but everything I had hoped for.

Almost despite myself,
my unanswered prayers were answered.

I am, among men, most richly blessed.

~ Roy Campanella
(American baseball player)

3.10 A Christmas Wish

This
Christmas
end a quarrel.
Seek out a forgotten
friend. Dismiss suspicion,
and replace it with trust...
Write a love letter. Share some
treasure. Give a soft answer. Encourage youth. Manifest your loyalty in
word and deed. Keep a promise. Find the
time. Forgo a grudge. Forgive an enemy. Listen.
Apologize if you were wrong. Try to understand.
Flout envy. Examine your demands on others. Think
first of someone else. Appreciate. Be kind, be gentle.
Laugh a little. Laugh a little more. Deserve confidence.
Take up arms against malice. Decry complacency. Express your
gratitude. Go to church. Welcome a stranger. Gladden the heart
of a child. Take pleasure in the beauty and wonder of the earth. Speak
your love. Speak
it again. Speak
it still once
again.

~ Unknown

3.11 Ten Rules for Being Human

1. You will receive a body.

    You may love it or hate it, but it will be yours for the duration of your life on Earth.

2. You will be presented with lessons.

    You are enrolled in a full-time informal school called *life*. Each day in this school you will have the opportunity to learn lessons. You may like the lessons or hate them, but you have designed them as part of your curriculum.

3. There are no mistakes, only lessons.

    Growth is a process of experimentation, a series of trials, errors, and occasional victories. The failed experiments are as much a part of the process as the experiments that work.

4. A lesson is repeated until learned.

    Lessons will be presented to you in various forms until you have learned them. When you have learned

SPIRITUAL WELLNESS

them, you can then go on to your next lesson. If you do not learn the easy lessons they become harder. You will know you have learned a lesson when your actions and outcomes change.

5. Learning does not end.

    There is no part of life that does not contain its lessons. Every person, every incident, is the universal teacher. If you are alive, there are lessons to be learned.

6. *There* is no better than *here*.

    Happiness is in the journey from *here* to *there*, not the destination itself. When your *there* has become a *here* you will simply obtain another *there* that will look better than *here*.

7. Others are merely mirrors of you.

    You cannot love or hate something about another person unless it reflects something you love or hate in yourself.

8. What you make of your life is up to you.

    You have all the tools and resources you need. What you do with them is up to you.

9. Your answers lie within you.

    All you need to do is look, listen, and trust.

10. You will forget all of this at birth. You can remember it if you want by unraveling the double helix of inner knowing.

~ Chérie Carter-Scott

(Author, *If Life Is a Game, These Are the Rules*)

3.12 On Being Hurt

I once heard a story about a man who was visiting his brother's house. He was playing with his little two-year-old nephew when suddenly the child hit him, perhaps out of playfulness or upset about something. The man's first instinct was to hit the little boy back, but then he paused for a moment and realized, "Wait a moment, this is just a little child who doesn't know any better . . . maybe he's confused or angry, but he may not know why."

As adults, when someone hurts us with words or actions, pause for a moment before you retaliate and consider the above. Is this person hurt or angry for some other reason, or just plain confused about what's going on in his or her life? Just because someone is an *adult* in human years doesn't mean they're a mature *grown-up*. Many adults I know are still acting like a confused, angry child. Once you realize this,

SPIRITUAL WELLNESS

it's easy to understand and forgive others' hurtful actions or words toward us.

Remember this: If someone's a cripple, can you get angry at them for not being able to run?

~ The Author

3.13 I Am Thankful for . . .

The partner who hogs the covers every night, because it means I am not alone.

The teenager who is not doing the dishes, but is watching TV, because it means he/she is at home and not on the streets.

For the taxes I pay, because it means I am employed.

For the mess to clean after a party, because it means I have been surrounded by friends.

For the clothes that fit a little snug, because it means I have enough to eat.

For a lawn that needs mowing, windows that need cleaning, and gutters that need fixing, because it means I have a home.

SPIRITUAL WELLNESS

For all the complaining I hear about the government,
because it means we have freedom of speech.

For the parking spot I find at the far end of the parking lot,
because it means I am capable of walking and have been
blessed with transportation.

For my huge heating bill, because it means I am warm.

For the lady behind me in church who sings off-key,
because it means I can hear.

For the pile of laundry and ironing,
because it means I have clothes to wear.

For weariness and aching muscles at the end of the day,
because it means I am capable of working hard.

For the alarm that goes off in the early morning hours,
because it means I am alive.

And finally . . . for too much email, because it means I
have friends who are thinking of me.

Count your blessings and be thankful for them.

~ UNKNOWN

3.14 Your Spiritual Journey

Be patient . . . in time you will receive an adequate explanation for every paradox.

The harvest of seeds sown in one lifetime are often not reaped in the same lifetime.

If you can return love instead of resentment and hate to anyone who injures you, you are released from the bondage of karma with that person.

Troubles, accidents, and tragedies are part of the natural process of soul development.

Accept all that happens to you as an outworking of divine law.

SPIRITUAL WELLNESS

The very best school for the pupil-disciple is everyday contact with ordinary people . . . the friction of daily life smooths the rough edges of our character.

So long as your life is spent in service, God will protect you. Whatever happens, all is well in the end.

The man of God learns to keep quiet and endeavors to help others by giving kindness and love to his fellows.

Pain is necessary for our soul development. It alerts us to things that are dangerous and wrong in our lives. Like a child touching a hot stove, we must learn the same way. Pain motivates us to find solutions to our problems. We do not move or grow unless we are uncomfortable. Coming out of pain into relief is one of life's joys. In an odd way, our enemies are also our benefactors—they are the first to point out our mistakes and weaknesses. Our friends and families push us to our limits; our enemies push us beyond.

Prayer works. Prayer is the act of asking God for help and guidance. Meditation is the act of waiting for an answer. You don't have to go to church to pray. In prayer, don't ask for *stuff*—like a new car, fame, money, and so forth. Ask that God's will, not yours, be done.

THE GOOD NEWS FILE

God may not always give us what we want but He always gives us what we need. Every day just do the best with whatever you've got, then turn it over to God.

~ Unknown

4.0
SERVICE

4.1 Acts of Random Kindness and the Ripple Effect

Back in the 1990s, there was a phrase that swept the nation—*Random Acts of Kindness*. It was everywhere, on TV ads, magazines, billboards, and subway walls. Its premise was simple: Just do something good for someone else, for no particular reason, and without thinking of getting anything back in return.

In 2000, there was the movie *Pay It Forward*. It was a story about a young boy given a homework assignment on how to improve his community. His solution? Do something good for three other people, then have each of those three help three other people, then have those three help three others, and so on. In the end, thousands in his community were positively affected.

In physics, there is the *ripple effect*. When an object is dropped in a pond the waves ripple outward until they hit the shore and bounce off, sometimes back to the center and sometimes in other directions. No matter how far away a shore may be, the wave will always rebound . . . even thousands of miles away.

How are these stories related and how do they affect those of us in Alcoholics and Narcotics Anonymous? Service to others is an important part of our recovery and healing process. By helping others, we accomplish two things. First, we help someone else with problems in their lives, thus making their lives better. Second, by focusing our minds and lives on someone other than ourselves we can forget our own problems, even momentarily. Acts of kindness ripple out as well. When people are treated well, they treat others the same way. If someone lets you into a busy traffic lane, you tend to let the next guy in, right?

Many people hesitate to give of their own time, money, and energy. Their first thought may often be: "What's in it for me?" or "How will I be repaid?" or "Am I losing something in my giving?" The Bible teaches us that the more we give the more we receive. My personal experience is that I usually get back twice what I give out. It may not come back immediately or in the same way I gave it out, but in the long run my service to others always returns manifold. It's a basic law of the universe. And if someone asks how they can repay me, I just say *pay it forward to someone else*.

Once we get over our fear and hesitancy of giving to others, it becomes easy. Our Higher Power knows and sees

SERVICE

everything we do for others. Nothing is ever forgotten. As we show love, mercy, and kindness to others, so will the universe return the same things to our own lives. It is a beautiful and consistent process. Just as the ripples from a single stone go out and return, so will our giving go out and affect the lives of other people. Give, give, and give some more. The more you give, the better you'll feel. You just have to trust the process. Never pass up an opportunity to help someone else and leave the world a better place every day.

~ The Author
(Recovering addict)

4.2 Acts of Service

In the end, all that's important is whether you've left the world a better place with your life. Each and every day try to be of service to others. Remember, when you die you can't take it with you (i.e., material wealth), so do whatever good you can while you're here. You will always be remembered more for your kindness and service to others than how much money or fame you had.

On helping others: You can never take care of anyone else until you first take care of yourself. Try to help others, but do not be consumed and destroyed by their problems. Your own mental, emotional, physical, and spiritual health should be your first priority. If you're sick or weak, you can never help others.

Never underestimate the power your words and actions may have on others around you. While you may feel small

SERVICE

and unimportant at times, you are very important to others. A kind word and helping hand can often make a big difference in others' lives. Any acts, no matter how small, are worth doing.

Be useful to somebody each and every day, and you'll never have a wasted day in your life.

Think globally and act locally is a favorite saying of environmentalists. Global change begins in our backyard; no matter what the needed change is. Yes, it's OK to worry about the Amazon rainforest, but better to plant trees in our own backyards. Don't depend on the president or Washington politicians to solve your problems. True change happens at the grassroot level and expands from there.

See one, do one, teach one is a frequently heard saying in medical school teaching. Take whatever you know, and pass it on to someone not as far on the road as you are.
~ THE AUTHOR

> *The greatest use of a life is to spend it on something that will outlast it.*
> ~ WILLIAM JAMES (1842–1910)
> (American philosopher)

> *A society grows great when men plant trees whose shade they know they shall never sit in.*
> ~ OLD GREEK PROVERB

THE GOOD NEWS FILE

Ask not what your country can do for you . . .
ask what you can do for your country.
~John F. Kennedy (1917–1963)
(35th U.S. President)

4.3 My Twenty-Foot Swath

I worried so much about world hunger today,
that I went home and ate five cookies.

Did personal or global problems ever become so overwhelming that you were immobilized, or driven to some action that actually aggravated the problem? Have you experienced such frustration about the hopelessness of solving the problems of poverty, environmental pollution, or human suffering that you could avoid it only by deciding that you were powerless to do anything about their alleviation? This is called *Responsibility Assumption Overload (RAO)*. Here's how I dealt with this feeling.

I park my car away from my building at work. That way I get both exercise and a parking space, as everyone else competes for spots next to the entrance. My morning and late afternoon strolls take me on a stretch of lawn between the tennis courts and the soccer field, and across an occasionally used softball diamond. The lawn is 20 feet wide, more or less. Soft and green, it was originally very littered. Tennis players discard tennis ball containers (and their flip-tops), worn-out sweat socks, broken shoelaces, and energy candy bar wrappers. Soccer game spectators leave behind beer bottles and junk food plastic.

In my early day, it disgusted me, and my thoughts centered on ways of correcting the situation: writing letters to the campus newspaper (no doubt totally ignored); campaigning for antilitter regulations (who would enforce them?); organizing a Zap-Day cleanup (leaving 364 days for littering). All my noble efforts would have demonstrated my indignation, raised my blood pressure, and attracted attention, but they would not have changed the appearance and/or condition of the area.

So, I decided to take ownership. I would be the solution. I did not tell anyone of this; it was probably against some rule or another. I decided that I would be responsible for the environmental quality of the 20-foot swath. I did not care what other parts of the campus were like. They were someone else's problem. But each day, going from and to my car, I picked up litter.

At first, it was as much as I could conveniently carry. Then I made a game of it, limiting my picking to ten items each way. It was an exciting day when I realized I was picking faster than *they* were littering. Finally, the great day arrived when I looked back on my 20 feet of lawn, now perfectly clean.

SERVICE

Where did I put the litter? At first, I brought it into a wastebasket in the building, or took it to the car to bring home. Then a curious thing happened. One day, large orange barrels appeared at each end of my swath. Someone in maintenance had become my silent conspirator—periodically emptying and replacing the barrels. He, too, knew the wisdom of keeping a low profile about it all.

I've done this for several years now. Has general campus appearance changed? Not much! Have litterers stopped littering? No! Then if nothing has changed, why bother?

Here lies the secret. Something *has* changed. My 20-foot swath—and I! That five-minute walk is a high spot of the day. Instead of fussing and stewing and storing up negative thoughts, I begin and end my workday in a positive mood. My perspective is brighter. I can enjoy my immediate surroundings—and myself—as I pass through a very special time and space.

It is better because of me. I am better because of *it*. *We* enjoy the relationship. Maybe, even, *it* looks forward with anticipation to my coming.

My learning, and the 20-foot swath, do not stop at the building door. There is an important principle that follows wherever I go. I cannot solve man's inhumanity to man, but I can affirm, with a smile and word of appreciation, to those who feel burdened by the need to work at lowly jobs. I cannot right the imbalances of centuries of discrimination, but I can *lift up* someone who feels the weight of poor self-image. I can treat women as equals without solving the problems of sex discrimination. I can seek out the social and economic litter in my own *20-foot swath* without demanding of myself that I *clean up the whole world*. As the Christopher Society says, "It is better to light one candle than to curse the darkness—and better to put on a pair of slippers than carpet the whole world."

I now practice a discipline of leaving each time-space capsule of my life a little better than when I entered it. Each personal contact, each event, each room I enter becomes a small challenge. I want to leave it improved, but more important, I am responsible to myself to be improved; and thereby, maybe—just maybe—my having been there will make life better for someone else.

I now have a 20-foot swath. Next year it may be 40, or 60, or 80 feet wide.

~ Kenneth V. Lundberg
(Oregon University professor)

5.0

SUCCESS

5.1 The Admiral's Lessons

An inspiring and powerful 20-minute commencement speech by Naval Admiral William H. McRaven, ninth commander of U.S. Special Forces Operations Command, at the university-wide commencement at the University of Texas at Austin on May 17, 2014.

Ten Life Lessons from Basic SEAL Training

1. **If you want to change the world, start off by making your bed.**
   If you can't do the little things right, you will never do the big things right.
2. **If you want to change the world, find someone to help you paddle.**
   You can't change the world alone—you will need some help—and to truly get from your starting

point to your destination takes friends, colleagues, the goodwill of strangers and a strong coxswain to guide them.

3. **If you want to change the world, measure a person by the size of their heart, not the size of their flippers.**

    SEAL training was a great equalizer. Nothing mattered but your will to succeed. Not your color, not your ethnic background, not your education, and not your social status.

4. **If you want to change the world, get over being a sugar cookie and keep moving forward.**

    Sometimes no matter how well you prepare or how well you perform you still end up as a sugar cookie.

    For failing the uniform inspection, you, the student [in Basic SEAL training], had to run, fully clothed, into the surf-zone and then, wet from head to toe, roll around on the beach until every part of your body was covered with sand. The effect was known as a *sugar cookie*. You stayed in that uniform the rest of the day—cold, wet, and sandy.

    There were many students who just couldn't accept the fact that all their effort was in vain . . . Those students didn't understand the purpose of the drill. You were never going to succeed. You were never going to have a perfect uniform.

5. **If you want to change the world, don't be afraid of the circuses.**

SUCCESS

Every day during training you were challenged with multiple physical events—long runs, long swims, obstacle courses, hours of calisthenics—something designed to test your mettle. Every event had standards—times you had to meet. If you failed to meet those standards your name was posted on a list, and at the end of the day those on the list were invited to a *circus*. A circus was two hours of additional calisthenics designed to wear you down, to break your spirit, to force you to quit.

Life is filled with circuses. You will fail. You will likely fail often. It will be painful. It will be discouraging. At times it will test you to your very core.

6. **If you want to change the world sometimes you have to slide down the obstacle headfirst.**
7. **If you want to change the world, don't back down from the sharks.**

There are a lot of sharks in the world. If you hope to complete the swim, you will have to deal with them.

8. **If you want to change the world, you must be your very best in the darkest moment.**

At the darkest moment of the mission is the time when you must be calm, composed—when all your tactical skills, your physical power, and all your inner strength must be brought to bear.

9. **If you want to change the world, start singing when you're up to your neck in mud.**

If I have learned anything in my time traveling the world, it is the power of hope. The power of one person—Washington, Lincoln, King, Mandela, and even a young girl from Pakistan, Malala—one person can change the world by giving people hope.

10. **If you want to change the world don't ever, ever ring the bell.**

    In SEAL training there is a bell. A brass bell that hangs in the center of the compound for all the students to see. All you have to do to quit—is ring the bell. Ring the bell and you no longer have to wake up at five o'clock. Ring the bell and you no longer have to do the freezing cold swims. Ring the bell and you no longer have to do the runs, the obstacle course, the PT—and you no longer have to endure the hardships of training. Just ring the bell. If you want to change the world don't ever, ever ring the bell.

...

Start each day with a task completed. Find someone to help you through life. Respect everyone. Know that life is not fair and that you will fail often. But if you take some risks, step up when the times are toughest, face down the bullies, lift up the downtrodden and never, ever give up—if you do these things, then the next generation and the generations that follow will live in a world far better than the one we have today.

SUCCESS

It matters not your gender, your ethnic or religious background, your orientation, or your social status. Our struggles in this world are similar, and the lessons to overcome those struggles and to move forward—changing ourselves and the world around us—will apply equally to all.

Changing the world can happen anywhere, and anyone can do it.

5.2 Success

To laugh often and much; to win the respect of intelligent people and affection of children; to earn the appreciation of honest critics and endure the betrayal of false friends; to appreciate beauty, to find the best in others; to leave the world a bit better, whether by a healthy child, a garden patch, or a redeemed social condition; to know even one life has breathed easier because you have lived. This is to have succeeded.

~ Ralph Waldo Emerson (1803–1882)
(American author)

SUCCESS

A Splendid Torch

I want to be thoroughly used up when I die,
for the harder I work, the more I live.
Life is no brief candle for me.
It is a sort of splendid torch which
I have got hold of for a moment,
And I want to make it burn as brightly
as possible before handing it on
to future generations.

~ GEORGE BERNARD SHAW (1856–1950)
(Irish author)

Throw yourself full throttle in the direction of what consumes your thoughts and ambitions—this is the true path to success.
~ SAMANTHA WILLS
(Australian businesswoman)

Never let your formal education get in the way of what you learn in the street.
~ JACK DAVIDSON
(Writer)

Fatigue makes cowards of us all.
~ VINCE LOMBARDI
(Football coach)

THE GOOD NEWS FILE

*Small efforts made frequently by many people
can make a world of difference.*
~ Margaret Mead
(Anthropologist)

From whom much is given, much is expected.
~ Unknown

Change is only positive when it benefits a majority of people.
~ Unknown

*God sends the necessary friends and helpers along the Road
of Life to love and help you—it may not be your blood family
(the ones you think would help you), but more often others.*
~ The Author

*Don't worry about tomorrow, the necessary
things will unfold as you need them.*
~ The Author

*Trust life, trust God, trust events, trust the serendipitous
appearance of special people into your life. Don't overanalyze or
sweat the details or dwell on the past. The way will be shown.*
~ White Eagle
(Spiritualist)

SUCCESS

Success is not final,
failure is not fatal.
~ **Winston Churchill** (1874–1965)
(British Prime Minister)

Know exactly what you want in any situation,
and the world will follow you.
~ **The Author**

Rejection in one situation is not meant to be equated with
failure—it sometimes is meant to push you in another direction.
~ **Unknown**

The world breaks everyone, and afterwards,
some are stronger at the broken places.
~ **Ernest Hemingway** (1899–1961)
(American novelist)

The achiever never knows whether he is succeeding
or failing, only that he is not finished.
~ **Chinese proverb**

All it takes is one right turn to make up for
all the wrong turns before in your life.
~ **The Author**

THE GOOD NEWS FILE

As long as you have a passion in life, a desire to learn, a curiosity for all things, a desire to travel and a sense of adventure, you will remain young.
~ THE AUTHOR

If you want friends, let others win and feel superior. The more arguments you win, the fewer friends you'll have.
~ THE AUTHOR

Blessed is the man with new worlds to conquer. For him the future beams with promise. Ahead of him there is always another dream castle glittering in the sun—and what fun it is to build foundations under them.
~ WHITE EAGLE
(Spiritualist)

Set yourself some goals of what you want to do in life, and make an effort to complete them so that when you look back on it all you can say is "Well, at least I tried."
~ UNKNOWN

There is something about giving to others that takes the spotlight off your own pain.
~ NORMAN VINCENT PEALE (1898–1993)
(American theologian)

SUCCESS

Always put yourself in others' shoes. If you feel that they hurt you, they probably hurt the other person as well.
~ THE AUTHOR

If God is for us, who can be against us?
~ ROMANS 8:31

Miracles, when aided and abetted by determined action, do happen.
~ ROBERT BRAULT
(Writer)

Function in disaster, finish in style.
~ STOCKARD CHANNING
(Actress)

I try not to focus on why something happens, rather I focus on what God wants me to do as a result of it.
~ LARRY BURKETT
(Christian radio personality)

If you can do a job a little better each day, you'll one day find you can do it better than anybody else.
~ FRANK ATHERTON
(British physician)

THE GOOD NEWS FILE

It's better to be a has-been than one who never was.
~ Unknown

If you have enough, you have everything.
~ Al Batt
(American humorist)

My definition of a rich man is never to be influenced by anyone, never to be under any time obligation, and to let nothing bother you. So, I'm still rich.
~ Peter McGill (1789-1860)
(Canadian businessman)

Maybe the ancients were right about it. A man's wealth can be measured by what he has; but it can also be measured by what he doesn't have and doesn't want. When he wants little, he is a rich man.
~ Chinese proverb

Keep a clear eye toward life's end. Do not forget your purpose and destiny as God's creature. What you are in His sight is what you are and nothing more. Remember that when you leave this earth, you can take with you nothing that you have received—fading symbols of honor, trappings of power—but only what you have given; a full heart enriched by honest service, love, sacrifice, and courage.
~ St. Francis of Assisi (1181–1226)
(Catholic saint)

SUCCESS

*Troubles are like weeds in a garden. We should
try to remove them, but if we concentrate only
on them, we miss the good things.*
~ BERT WILLIAMS (1874–1922)
(American entertainer)

Solitude is the price of greatness and advanced souls.
~ CHINESE PROVERB

*The ultimate of being successful is the luxury of giving
yourself the time to do what you want to do.*
~ LEONTYNE PRICE
(American soprano)

When you carry a load for a long time, you become strong.
~ UNKNOWN

*Let us not bankrupt our todays by paying interest
on the regrets of yesterday, or by borrowing
in advance the troubles of tomorrow.*
~ RALPH W. STOCKMAN (1889–1970)
(Christian minister)

Perform the work that is placed before you well and with grace.
~ UNKNOWN

THE GOOD NEWS FILE

The secret of change is to focus all of your energy, not on fighting the old, but on building the new.
~ SOCRATES (469–399 BC)
(Greek philosopher)

The journey of a thousand miles begins with the first step.
~ LAO TZU
(Chinese philosopher)

I will charge thee nothing but the promise that thee will help the next man thee finds in trouble.
~ MENNONITE PROVERB

The heart that is truly happy never grows old. We don't cease playing because we have grown old; we grow old because we cease playing.
~ DR. FRANK S. CAPRIO
(American jurist)

Don't miss the beautiful colors of the rainbow while you're looking for the pot of gold at the end of it.

~ BERN WILLIAMS (1929–2003)
(British philosopher)

SUCCESS

To find out what one is fitted to do and to secure an opportunity to do it is the key to happiness.

~ JOHN DEWEY (1859–1952)
(American psychologist)

You know what sophistication is basically? It's just the art of admitting that the unexpected is just what you anticipated.
~ SOPHIA LOREN
(Italian actress)

First and foremost, forgive and go easy on yourself.
~ BOB SCHUMACHER
(friend)

Success is doing fewer things better, leaving your mark on whatever you do; and understanding that there are no such things as coincidences.
~ UNKNOWN

We all become what we focus and dwell upon. Focus on the good and we will become good. Focus on negativity and that will be your reality.
~ THE AUTHOR

THE GOOD NEWS FILE

As the gardener, by severe pruning, forces the sap out of the tree into one or two more vigorous limbs, so should you stop off your miscellaneous activities and concentrate your force on one or a few points.
~ RALPH WALDO EMERSON (1803–1882)
(American essayist)

Hatred is not diminished by hatred at any time. Hatred is diminished by love—this is the eternal law.
~ THE DHAMMAPADA
(Buddhist scripture)

An expert is a person who has made all the mistakes that can be made in a very narrow field.
~ NIELS BOHR (1885–1962)
(Danish physicist)

If you have much, give of your wealth; if you have little, give of your heart.
~ ARAB PROVERB

Thank God every morning when you get up that you have something to do which must be done, whether you like it or not. Being forced to work, and forced to do your best, will breed in you temperance and self-control, diligence and strength of will, cheerfulness and content, and a hundred virtues which the idle never know.

SUCCESS

~ CHARLES KINGSLEY (1819–1875)
(Church of England priest)

It isn't how much you know but what you get done that the world rewards and remembers.
~ ALFRED A. MONTAPERT (1906–1997)
(American philosopher)

Will your current problems really matter five years down the road? That's a good question to ask when you're bothered by a traffic jam or an argument. Don't allow minor setbacks or concerns to get in the way of concentrating on what's important.
~ THE AUTHOR

Remember that life is not measured in hours, but in accomplishments.
~ JAMES A. PIKE (1913–1969)
(American Episcopal priest)

Judge each day not by the harvest you reap but by the seeds you plant.
~ WILLIAM ARTHUR WARD (1921–1994)
(American motivational speaker)

Work like you don't need the money, love like you've never been hurt, and dance like you do when nobody's watching.
~ ANONYMOUS BUMPER STICKER

THE GOOD NEWS FILE

All trials we face lead us to our purpose.
~ **CHINESE PROVERB**

Success is sometimes a series of failures held together by the strong bonds of determination and persistence.
~ **WILLIAM ARTHUR WARD (1921–1994)**
(American motivational writer)

When you want something done; assign it . . . monitor it, then do it yourself.
~ **ROBERT HALF**
(American job services)

The best preparation for tomorrow is to do today's work superbly well.
~ **WILLIAM OSLER (1849–1919)**
(Physician)

Obstacles are those frightful things you see when you take your eyes off your goal.
~ **HENRY FORD (1863–1947)**
(American automobile industrialist)

A small trouble is like a pebble. Hold it too close to your eye, and it fills the whole world and puts everything out of focus. Hold it at proper viewing distance, and it can be examined and properly classified. Throw it

SUCCESS

at your feet, and it can be seen in its true setting, just one more tiny bump on the pathway to eternity.
~ CELIA LUCE (1914–2008)
(U.S. writer)

Stress is God-given. It crystallized your whole thought. I'm much smarter onstage than off. Sheer panic is the greatest thing for all of us.
~ CAROL CHANNING
(Actress)

Nothing can resist an idea whose time has come.
~ VICTOR HUGO (1802–1885)
(French novelist)

A candle loses nothing by lighting another candle.
~ FATHER JAMES KELLER (1900–1977)
(Founder, The Christophers)

Wealth consists not in having possessions but in having few wants.
~ ESTHER DE WAAL
(Writer)

It does not matter how slow you go, as long as you do not stop.
~ CONFUCIUS (551–479 BC)
(Chinese philosopher)

THE GOOD NEWS FILE

*We make a living by what we get—but
we make a life by what we give.*
~ Winston Churchill (1874–1965)
(British Prime Minister)

*May you have enough happiness to make you sweet,
enough trials to make you strong, enough sorrow to
keep you human, enough hope to make you happy.*
~ Unknown

*Be decisive. Right or wrong, make a decision. The road of life
is paved with flat squirrels who couldn't make a decision.*
~ Unknown

Embrace ambiguity and trust your gut.
~ Unknown

*It is the greatest wealth to live a frugal
life with a contented mind.*
~ Lucretius (99–55 BC)
(Roman philosopher/poet)

*Life's direct experience is more important
than formal education.*
~ Unknown

SUCCESS

*Pray as though everything depended on God.
Work as though everything depended on you.*
~ St. Augustine (354–430)
(Roman theologian)

On passion—Where your heart is, there is your treasure.
~ Luke 12:34

*A man who is self-reliant, positive, optimistic, and undertakes
his work with the assurance of success, magnetizes his condition.
He draws to himself the creative powers of the universe.*
~ Rev. Norman Vincent Peale (1898–1993)
(American theologian)

*The happiest of people don't necessarily have the
best of everything; they just make the most of
everything that comes along their way.*
~ Unknown

Lead your life with quiet magnificence.
~ Confucius

*They may forget what you said, but they will
never forget how you made them feel.*
~ Reverend Robert Schuller
(American theologian)

THE GOOD NEWS FILE

It hurts to find out that what you wanted doesn't match what you dreamed it would be.
~ Randy K. Milholland
(American author)

It's easy to be ethical when you have enough money, but when you're poor your ethics can go out the window.
~ The Author

If you plant a tree, don't keep pulling it up by the roots to see how it's growing.
~ Johnny Appleseed
(American legend)

When you realize you have a problem, you never know how God will manifest in your life. You need to go into your heart and say, "Use me. I am your channel. I am your instrument. Give me some guidance." What happens then is astounding. You hardly have to do anything. You just have to be willing to act when the inspiration comes or when the signal comes. Then you are led to all kinds of circumstances that are absolutely unbelievable.
~ Dennis Weaver
{American actor)

Many people wait for their ship to come in, but forget that they must first dredge the harbor, build a

SUCCESS

lighthouse and a pier, so the ship can find them and dock. If they don't, their ship will find another port.
~ JOHN COLUMBUS
(Radio broadcaster)

Success is a journey, not a destination.
~ JACK DAVIDSON
(American author)

Treat each day as if it were your last and live it to the fullest. And pretend that you have only six months to live— would you really worry about your current problems?
~ THE AUTHOR

Each of us is born with the potential for 2,700,000,000 heartbeats, so don't waste any of them!
—YOUR PHYSICIAN AUTHOR

5.3 Mistakes

The Gutenberg Slip

Making mistakes is part of being human. The good part about mistakes is that it shows we're at least trying to work on projects or improving our lives in some way. It's OK to make mistakes as long as we learn from them, but if you make the same mistake more than two or three times, it only shows you're not paying attention. Thomas Edison, one of the world's greatest inventors, failed over ten thousand times in his quest to develop the incandescent light bulb before he found the right formula.

One of the most important "mistakes" in human history was made by Johannes Gutenberg (1400–1468), a German printer, goldsmith, inventor, and publisher living in Frankfurt, Germany. He introduced printing to Europe with his mechanical, movable-type printing press. His work started the

SUCCESS

Printing Revolution, ushering in the modern period of human history. It played a key role in the development of the Renaissance, Reformation, Age of Enlightenment, and Scientific Revolution, as well as laying the material basis for the modern knowledge-based economy and the spread of learning to the masses (Wikipedia).

Before Gutenberg, books were printed on wooden blocks. Each page had to be carved into a single block, which often required days to finish. The block would then be inked and pressed onto the paper. Each block could be used to print only about a hundred pages, after which it had to be discarded.

Legend has it that one day he was working in his shop, carving a block, when something remarkable happened. He'd been sick for several days and was coughing and sneezing, when during one bad cough his hand slipped and cut the block into several pieces. He panicked and was distraught at the seeming destruction of several days' work. No longer able to work, he went home and cried for days.

When he returned several days later, he looked at his seemingly destroyed work and noticed something interesting. Several of the cuts had resulted in individual letters, and he realized they could now be rearranged into words. He then cut up the remaining wooden block into individual letters, and used them to recreate an entire page of words. This was his "eureka" moment.

So, when seeming disaster happens and a valued project falls apart, don't panic. Take a break for a couple of days and let your subconscious work on a possible solution, then return for a new perspective on your work. No mistakes (or coincidences) happen in God's world—they are His way of bringing the necessary people, books, and ideas into your life. And, with each mistake, make sure you learn from it.

Wait for your Gutenberg moment!

~ The Author

5.4 Success and Failure
by Napoleon Hill
(naphill.org)

Napoleon Hill was a young man who spent over two decades studying the lives, thoughts, and business practices of some of the most successful and wealthy men at the beginning of the 20th century. Among them were Andrew Carnegie, Henry Ford, and John D. Rockefeller. After decades of research, he wrote the best-selling book *Think and Grow Rich*. The Napoleon Hill Foundation continues his work and offers daily inspirational guidance. All quotes are from Napoleon Hill's writings.

Failure is a blessing when it pushes us out of a cushioned sense of self-satisfaction and forces us to do something useful.

Failure is not a disgrace if you have sincerely done your best.

THE GOOD NEWS FILE

No one can keep you down but yourself.

*Great advances in knowledge are often achieved
by people with an almost fanatical devotion
to finding the solution to a problem.*

There is a vast difference between failure and temporary defeat.

*Victory is always possible for the person
who refuses to stop fighting.*

*Only those who have the habit of going the second
mile ever find the end of the rainbow.*

*Remember the mind grows strong through use.
Struggle makes power.*

*If you don't know why you failed, you are
no wiser than when you began.*

*Failure is a trickster with a keen sense of irony and cunning.
It takes great delight in tripping one when
success is almost within reach.*

*Failure seems to be nature's way for preparing
us for great responsibilities.*

SUCCESS

CRISIS: The turning point in the lives of those who succeed usually comes at the moment of some crisis, through which they are introduced to their other selves.

Your failure may prove to be an asset, provided you know why you failed.

Great achievement is born of struggle. As Ralph Waldo Emerson once said, "Our strength grows out of our weakness—not until we are pricked and stung and sorely shot at, does the indignation awaken, which arms itself with secret forces."

Your real courage shows best in the hour of adversity.

Courage is not the absence of fear, but moving forward in spite of it.

Even when you encounter your first serious blow, you can never lose two of the most important assets you have. These are the power of your mind and your freedom to use it. Remember, no matter where you are now, whatever you can conceive and believe, you can achieve.

When adversity overtakes you, it pays to be thankful it was not worse instead of worrying over your misfortune.

THE GOOD NEWS FILE

God never gives us more than we can handle.

*If life hands you a lemon, don't complain,
but instead make lemonade
to sell to those who are thirsty from complaining.*

*If you have no major purpose,
you are drifting toward certain failure.
Unless a ship has a good rudder, it will drift endlessly.*

*Anyone can quit when the going is hard, but a
thoroughbred never quits until he wins.*

*Many successful people have found opportunities
in failure and adversity that they could not
recognize in more favorable circumstances.*

*Before opportunity crowns you with great success,
it usually tests your mettle through adversity.*

*READINESS: Psychologists have correctly said that when
one is truly ready for a thing, it puts in its appearance.*

*Knowledge will not attract money unless it is organized,
and intelligently directed, through practical plans of action,
to the definite end of accumulation
of money.*

SUCCESS

Honesty and hard work are commendable traits of character, but they will never make a success of the person who does not guide them toward a definite major purpose. A major purpose and outstanding character are a formidable combination.

You can tell by the company people choose what sort of character they have.

If you are sure you are right, you need not worry about what the world thinks.

Constancy of purpose is the first principle of success. Discipline and the willpower to succeed are the second.

Great fortunes and modest fortunes are a blessing only when they are used in good part to benefit others.

When the going is hardest, just keep on going on, and you'll get there sooner than someone who finds the going easy.

Opportunity has a queer way of stalking the person who can recognize it and is ready to embrace it.

Willpower is the outgrowth of definiteness of purpose expressed through persistent action, based on personal initiative. As Coach Darryl Royal once said, "Luck is where preparation meets opportunity."

THE GOOD NEWS FILE

Opportunity never sneaks up on those who straddle the fence of indecision.

A positive mental attitude is an irresistible force that knows no such thing as an immovable body.

Your progress begins in your own mind and ends in the same place. No one can keep you down but yourself.

FOLLOWERS: Most great leaders begin in the capacity of followers. They became great leaders because they were intelligent followers.

Just what are you waiting for and why are you waiting?

Everything you create or acquire begins in the form of desire.

Opportunity has many tricks. It has a sly way of slipping in by the back door, and often it comes disguised in the form of misfortune, or temporary defeat. Perhaps that is why so many fail to recognize it when it comes.

Remember, your mental limitations are of your own making. As Robert Browning once said, "A man's reach should exceed his grasp . . . or what's a heaven for?"

SUCCESS

When the plan comes through to your conscious mind, accept it with appreciation and gratitude—and act on it at once. Do not hesitate.

You will never be greater than the thoughts that dominate your mind. Remember, small minds think about things, great minds think about ideas.

Those who will not take a chance seldom have one thrust upon them. No one on earth is going to force success upon you; you will find it only to the degree that you actively seek it out.

The richest persons are those who give most in service.

Your true age is determined by your mental attitude, not the years you have lived.

The safest and best way to punish one who has done you an injustice is to do him or her a kind deed in return.

Only the highway of useful service leads to the city of happiness.

Watch the one ahead of you, and you'll learn why he is ahead. Then emulate him.

The world stands aside and makes room for the person who knows where he's going and is on his way.

THE GOOD NEWS FILE

BELIEF: There is a difference between wishing for a thing and being ready for it.

No one is ready for a thing unless he believes he can acquire it.

The keenest minds are the ones that have been whetted by practical experience.

This is a fine world for the person who knows precisely what he or she expects from life and is busy getting it.

It isn't defeat but rather your mental attitude toward it that whips you. Defeat is never permanent unless you allow it to be so.

If you are really great, you will let others discover this fact from your actions. Make it a habit to demonstrate your abilities before talking about them.

Instead of complaining about what you don't like about your job, start commending what you do like and see how quickly it improves. Make it a point to find something good in your job.

A blind boy paid his way to a master's degree at Northwestern University by taking notes on class lectures in Braille, typing them, and selling copies to classmates with stronger eyes

SUCCESS

but weak ambition. It all hinges on determination. If you have the will to succeed you will somehow find a way.

Faith is a combination of thoughts and actions. It is the belief in things unseen. When you apply your faith in yourself, your faith in your fellow man, and your faith in God, the result is a positive course of action that when persistently followed will almost always lead to success.

Medals and titles will not count when you get to heaven, but you may be looked over carefully for the sorts of deeds you have done. In the afterlife, the only real measure of success will be how you have lived your life, not how much money you have accumulated.

If you have something you don't need, give it to someone who needs it. It will come back to you in one way or another. The community in which you live will become a better place and you will be happier being a part of it.

You can't control others' acts, but you can control your reaction to their acts, and that is what counts most to you. No one can make you feel any negative emotion—fear, anger, or inferiority—without your express permission.

Good intentions are useless until they are expressed in appropriate action. The most mediocre idea

THE GOOD NEWS FILE

acted upon is far more valuable than a flash of genius that resides only in your mind.

Most failures could have been converted into successes if someone had held on another minute or made more effort. Without adversity, you would never develop the qualities of reliability, loyalty, humility, and perseverance that are so essential to enduring success.

Success attracts success and failure attracts failure because of the law of harmonious attraction. Negative people attract only other negative people, while positive thinkers attract like-minded individuals. Train your mind to visualize yourself acquiring a specific amount of wealth or achieving a certain goal—whatever you most desire. You come finally to believe anything you tell yourself often enough—even if it is not true. Your subconscious mind will eventually begin to accept it as fact.

The con man works harder and pays more for what he gets out of life than any other person, but he kids himself into believing he is getting something for nothing. A deal is a good one only when it is good for everyone involved.

A burning desire to be and to do is the starting point from which the dreamer must take off.

SUCCESS

You cannot make all people like you, but you can rob them of a sound reason for disliking you. Self-respect will mean far more to you than mere popularity.

Nature yields her most profound secrets to those who are most determined to uncover them.

Most illness begins with a negative mind. Hypochondriacs, people who are convinced they are sick, even though nothing is wrong with them, experience the exact symptoms of the actual illness. Make sure you feed your mind with plenty of positive thoughts.

Failure seems to be nature's plan for preparing us for great responsibilities. Failure allows us to develop the essential humility—necessary when we ultimately achieve greatness.

Are you waiting for success, or are you going out to find it? If you are waiting for success to seek you out, you are headed for a big disappointment. You must prepare for it and actively seek it out if you ever plan to achieve any measure of success in your life.

Everything you create or acquire begins in the form of desire. The secret to action is a red-hot desire.

THE GOOD NEWS FILE

As the great baseball manager Branch Rickey once said, "Luck is the residue of design."

Don't wait for something to happen—make it happen!

Unlimited power may be available when two or more people coordinate their thoughts and actions in a spirit of perfect harmony for the attainment of a definite purpose. Align yourself with people whose strengths complement yours.

There is always a shortage of people who get the job done on time without excuses or grumbling.

By all means tell the world how good you are— but share the credit and reserve the blame.

Control your mind, and you may never be controlled by the mind of another.

A lazy individual is either sick or has not found the work that he or she likes best.

Success requires no explanation; failures must be doctored with alibis.

No one can succeed and remain successful without the friendly cooperation of others.

SUCCESS

Profanity is a sign of inadequate vocabulary or unsound judgment—or both. Mark Twain once observed that the difference between the right word and the almost-right word is the difference between lightning and lightning bug. It is never appropriate to use profanity, especially among people you do not know. Instead, build your vocabulary by reading and studying every day.

The greatest cure known is WORK. Emotions will always respond to action. If you have feelings of loneliness or discouragement the best way to kill such negative emotions is to work them to death. There's nothing like a hard day of physical work to put everything in proper perspective.

I hope this wealth of Napoleon Hill's wisdom has helped you.

~ THE AUTHOR

5.5 Boldness

Concerning all acts of
initiative and creation there is
one elementary truth the ignorance
of which kills countless ideas and
splendid plans; that the moment one
definitely commits oneself, then
Providence moves too. All sorts of
things occur to help one that would
otherwise not have occurred.
A whole stream of events issues from
the decision, raising in one's favor
all manner of unforeseen incidents
and meetings and material assistance
which no man could have dreamed
would have come his way.
As Goethe said, "Whatever you

SUCCESS

can do, or dream you can do,
do it. Boldness has genius,
power, and magic in it.
Begin it now."

~ W. H. Murray
(Scottish mountaineer)

Throw yourself full throttle in the direction of what consumes your thoughts and ambitions.
~ Samantha Wills
(Australian jeweler)

5.6 A Commencement Address

Imagine life as a game in which you are juggling five balls in the air. You name them . . . Work, Family, Health, Friends, Spirit, and you're keeping all these in the air. You will soon realize work is a rubber ball. If you drop it, it will bounce back. But the other four balls—family, health, friends, and spirit are made of glass. If you drop one of these, they will be irrevocably scuffed, marked, nicked, damaged, or even shattered. They will never be the same. You must understand that and strive for balance in your life.

How?

1. Don't undermine your worth by comparing yourself with others. It is because we are different that each of us is special.
2. Don't set your goals by what others deem important. Only you know what is best for you.

SUCCESS

3. Don't take for granted the things closest to your heart. Cling to them as you would your life, for without them, life is meaningless.
4. Don't let your life slip through your fingers by living in the past, or for your future. By living your life one day at a time, you live ALL the days of your life.
5. Don't give up when you still have something to give. Nothing is really over until the moment you stop trying.
6. Don't be afraid to admit that you are less than perfect. It is this fragile thread that binds us together.
7. Don't be afraid to encounter risks. It is by taking chances that we learn how to be brave.
8. Don't shut love out of your life by saying it's impossible to find. The quickest way to receive love is to give it; the fastest way to lose love is to hold it too tightly; and the best way to keep love is to give it wings.
9. Don't run through life so fast you forget not only where you've been, but also where you are going.
10. Don't forget that a person's greatest emotional need is to feel appreciated.
11. Don't be afraid to learn. Knowledge is weightless; a treasure you can always carry easily.
12. Don't use time or words carelessly. Neither can be retrieved.
13. Life is not a race, it's a journey to be savored each step of the way. Yesterday is history. Tomorrow is a

mystery, and Today is a gift and that's why we call it "the present."

~ Brian G. Dyson
(CEO, Coca-Cola)

5.7 All I Ever Really Needed to Know I Learned in Kindergarten

Most of what I really need to know about how to live and what to do and how to be, I learned in kindergarten. Wisdom was not at the top of the graduate mountain, but there in the sandbox at nursery school.

These are the things I learned: Share everything. Play fair. Don't hit people. Put things back where you found them. Clean up your own mess. Don't take things that aren't yours. Say you're sorry when you hurt somebody. Wash your hands before you eat. Flush. Warm cookies and cold milk are good for you. Lead a balanced life. Learn some and think some and draw and paint and sing and dance and play and work every day some.

Take a nap every afternoon. When you go out into the world, watch for traffic, hold hands, and stick together. Be aware of wonder. Remember the little seed in the plastic cup. The roots go down and the plant goes up and nobody really knows how or why, but we are all like that. Goldfish and hamsters and white mice and even the little seed in the plastic cup—they all die. So do we.

And then remember the book about Dick and Jane and the first word you learned, the biggest word of all: LOOK. Everything you need to know is in there somewhere. The Golden Rule and love and basic sanitation. Ecology and politics and sane living.

Think of what a better world it would be if we all—the whole world—had cookies and milk about three o'clock every afternoon and then lay down with our blankets for a nap. Or if we had a basic policy in our nations to always put things where we found them and cleaned up our own messes. And it is still true, no matter how old you are, when you go out into the world it is better to hold hands and stick together.

~ **Robert Fulghum**
(American author)

5.8 Attitude

The longer I live the more I realize the impact of attitude on life. Attitude, to me, is more important than facts.

It is more important than the past, than education, than money, than circumstances, than failures, than successes, than what other people think or say or do.

It is more important than appearance, giftedness, or skill.

It will make or break a company—a church, a home.

The remarkable thing is we have a choice every day regarding the attitude we will embrace for that day.

We cannot change our past . . . we cannot change the fact that people will act in a certain way.

We cannot change the inevitable. The only thing we can do is play on the one string we have, and that is our attitude.

I am convinced that life is 10 percent what happens to me and 90 percent how I react to it.

THE GOOD NEWS FILE

And so it is with you . . .
we are in charge of our Attitudes.
~ CHARLES SWINDOLL
(Christian pastor)

6.0

MEN AND WOMEN

6.1 On Marriage

Behind every great man is a great woman.

For guys: When you get serious with a girl make sure to spend plenty of time with and get to know her mother, because that's what the girl's going to be like in 25 years (same for women—get to know your guy's father well).

For guys: A woman's love is like a fire . . . it may start slowly (unlike a man's, which can start fast) and take a long time to build, but once it's going it can become a powerful force over time. Do not start a woman's fire—with pretty words and shiny trinkets—unless you are willing to take responsibility for wherever it goes and whatever it becomes. A woman's love can be one of the most powerful forces in your life, and in the universe, so don't take it lightly. It can be a force for good or a force for bad. And if you shun a woman, remember this: "Hell hath no fury like a woman scorned."

Men are characterized by three things—Mind, Energy, and Will.

Women are characterized by—Love, Nurturing, and Wisdom.

Never underestimate how fierce a woman can be. Under that pretty face can lie a will of steel. It has been said that one of the most powerful forces in the world is a mother defending her young. Also, in the ancient world, it was a common practice of many tribes to hand over their prisoners of war to the women of their tribe.

Men, too, deserve to be spoiled, told they are handsome, told their efforts are appreciated, and should also be made to feel secure. If he treats you like a queen, treat him like a king.

Men marry their "mothers" and women marry their "fathers."

Anyone who thinks a successful relationship and marriage is being happy 24 hours a day, seven days a week and 365 days a year is sorely mistaken. The amount of time spent together is not as important as the quality of time spent together. Some of the most successful marriages are in the navy and merchant marine—where one of the couple is gone six months a year. When they're together, they can enjoy their togetherness, and when apart, pursue their individual interests as well. In the Hopi Indian families, the man is often gone three to four days a week while out hunting, gathering, and so forth.

Never think that getting married is going to solve your problems, or be your only source of happiness. If anything, your problems will only change and maybe even worsen. Same thing with thinking that having a baby will fix a bad marriage. Marriage should be the icing on the cake of your life—not the cake itself. Yes, it's OK to marry somebody who *completes* you and fills in your weak spots. The ideal relationship is where the man's strong points complement the woman's weak points, and the woman's strengths complement the man's weak spots. A loving partner can be a wonderful source of strength and happiness in your life.

Advice to a young couple contemplating marriage: Never get married until you've spent at least six months together (preferably twelve). The first six months are the magical period . . . the classic honeymoon time. Everything is blissful. The sex is wonderful . . . anytime and anyplace. You find each other endlessly fascinating and the conversation is nonstop. At the beginning of the seventh month, you suddenly notice that your partner has a pimple on their butt and makes a funny noise while eating (which didn't used to bother you). The *Mickleson Rule* states that all relationships have a six-month lifespan . . . after that you'd better be good friends to start with or it isn't going to last. As hard as it for me to admit that my parents were right when they said you should be friends first, then lovers later—they were right.

Two things that a couple need to do before getting married . . . tend a garden together for six to twelve months, and wallpaper a house.

~ The Author

The best place for a man to meet a woman is working in the wheat fields, not at a Saturday night dance.
~ Old Slovak proverb

If it flies, floats, or fornicates . . . rent it, don't buy it.
~ Advice from a thrice-divorced Anchorage gynecologist

"What do women want?" is the single most frequently asked question among men. There is never a single good answer, and it all depends on how well you know your lady. Women are like weather systems—some days are nice and some days are rainy. If your lady is in a good mood, run with it and enjoy the day. If she's in a bad mood, just put on your *raincoat* and do something else, like working on your hobbies.

MEN AND WOMEN

I once dated a very nice lady and asked her the question of what women want. Her answer? "Much of the time we women really don't know what we want." As a final point, it's a well-known fact that one of the main reasons men go bald is trying to figure out women ... and pulling their hair out in the process!

In the end, a relationship with a good man or woman can be one of the best experiences of your life. It isn't easy, and takes work and compromise, but if you find the right person it can be wonderful. The career you choose and the person you marry are the two most important decisions of your adult life. Never give up your search for that someone special—always keep looking. Expect some rejections but remember it's a lot like fishing—you need to keep throwing your hook in the water. Don't take rejection personally (much easier said than done). Don't go for wealth; even that fades away. Don't always go after the best-looking person, either. Good looks can deceive. Look for someone who smiles and winks at you and makes your heart smile as well. A smile can make a dark day seem bright. There's almost always someone out there for you—just be patient.

For guys: Romancing a woman is a marathon, not a sprint. Expect setbacks along the way. Women need to be frequently assured that we love them, so saying, "I love you" once a year won't cut it.

THE GOOD NEWS FILE

For guys: Learn to love shopping, talking about your feelings, and saying "I'm sorry" (for things often completely unknown to you).

For guys: When dating, always remember that girls are just as scared and nervous as you are. I never had a sister so for the longest time I held women on a pedestal, rarely realizing that they sit on a toilet just like we guys do.

When women say they want to talk about a problem, what they really want is only for you to listen sympathetically—and not to hear your own ideas on how to solve it. When a wife wants to talk about a problem, most guys jump right into their *problem-solving mode*, and don't understand she just wants to be heard. During marriage counseling for my own failing marriage, I kept offering what I thought were great solutions, but my wife (and the group) seemed oddly unimpressed by my wonderful ideas.

There's a special way you need to listen to a woman . . . every 10 to 20 seconds just say "Uh-huh," or "Oh really?" or "I understand," or "That's terrible." This is not meant to sound shallow or calculating, rather it's a way to let your wife know that you're actively listening. Women just want to be heard, not advised. Try it—it works. When women talk it is an exchange of feelings and emotions and random stuff. When guys talk it's an exchange of facts and solutions.

MEN AND WOMEN

On living with a woman: Any man who lives with a woman for more than six months slowly and ultimately learns that it is the female who sets the rules and standards for their living space. It is a slow and subtle process but very real. In the farming industry they call it *domestication*. If the female is loving, she will do this with kindness and diplomacy, and the process isn't so bad. If, however, she isn't kind and loving it can be a slow descent into a living hell—as in "Honey, why can't my friends come over anymore—I thought you liked them." And for some couples, the household becomes a constant power struggle, with the male often losing and only wanting the stress to stop.

In a family, if you ask the kids who runs the house they will often say, "Well, Dad pays the bills but Mom runs the house." The problem with house rules is they are neither spoken nor written down. You can't say to your wife, "Honey, what are the rules . . . please tell me so I can follow them," because the very act of asking implies (in the female's mind) that if you really loved her you'd already know what the rules are. The only way you learn the rules is by (unintentionally) breaking them and suffering the consequences. This is the type of female thinking that drives men batty. So, ladies, if you love your guy, just tell him how you'd like things to be, and don't expect him to read your mind, OK? The husband/father is often relegated to a less dominant role in the household but should never stop exhibiting the strong male force that is needed for the stability of a home.

The feminist revolution was based on some important ideas and needed changes, like equal pay for equal work and no sexual harassment at work. However, the process also ended up making many young women feel guilty and giving them the feeling that the traditional roles of wife and mother were somehow neither important nor desired as a life choice. We now have over three generations of women who chose work over family. These women now have high-paying jobs and corporate power, but often live alone with their cats in their penthouse apartment, with no family and few friends in their drive to the top. Women of that period (and even continuing today), often claim that they want "more." More what? When I hear young women today talking like they're still an oppressed minority, I have to laugh. Do they not understand the incredible power women have had through history? Women control two of the most important areas of life—the home, and the sex life of a couple. Are these not incredible sources of power? A man cannot force himself on his woman until she is ready, and in the mood. Otherwise, it's called rape. Hopefully, however, the wife will understand the need for continued intimacy to maintain the strong bonds of the marriage and keep her husband happy.

It strikes me as odd that we (i.e., society) have been putting the cart before the horse by saying that love comes first, then sex. The wonderful feeling you get from having sex with your beloved *makes* you want to love and take care of him/her—for a long time.

Listen to your wife—she can often sniff out evil and both good and bad people.

The man must lead—the moon can only reflect what the sun shines. If the male shows strength, courage, and confidence, the female will feel safe, secure, protected, and loved—and able to show her loving and nurturing nature.

Marriage is, as I found out very quickly, not just about love and romance. It is also a binding, legal, and business contract, based on the presumption that both husband and wife are contributing equally to the financial success of the family. While awkward in the early, passionate phase of a romance, prenups make a lot of sense and can protect you from great hassles later on. The legal system doesn't care what the reality of the marriage is, it just assumes the whole deal's been 50/50.

Marriage should be mutually supportive and inspirational.

You shouldn't get married until you're fairly complete in your own development. You don't want to be a burden on your partner. Get your travel and adventures in during your 20s before you get serious. Once the kids start coming, you won't have the free time you used to have. You don't want to say, "Oh, I wish I had done that," after you settle down.

The person who has the least interest in a relationship has the greater power.

Women—the minute you stop caring about them they come running back.

Give love without expectation of return.
~ The Author

An ounce of love is worth a pound of knowledge.
~ John Wesley
(English theologian)

The heart has its own reasons which reason knows nothing of.
~ Blaise Pascal (1623–1662)
(French philosopher)

Love—the only way you can keep it is to give it away.

There is one love in every person's life against which all others are compared and judged.
~ The Author

MEN AND WOMEN

*The best way to cure a woman of anything is
to tell her it's caused by advancing age.*
~ DEBBY BOONE
(Entertainer)

*For couples: Never stop dating each other.
Once a week have a regular date night.*
~ REV. ROBERT SCHULLER
(Theologian)

*Clever and attractive women do not want to vote; they are
willing to let men govern as long as they govern men.*
~ GEORGE BERNARD SHAW (1856–1950)
(Irish playwright)

*Giving someone all your love is never an
assurance that they'll love you back. Don't expect
love in return; just wait for it to grow in their heart,
but if it doesn't, be content it grows in yours.*

On keeping a man happy: I once talked to an older lady who'd had a long and successful marriage and asked her, "How do you keep a man happy?" Her answer, "It's not complicated . . . just make him a good hot meal every day, and make love to him several times a week." Ladies, if you don't want your man to stray, then keep him happy so that his home life is better than anything he can find outside the home.

THE GOOD NEWS FILE

For guys: If you're seeking a good woman, clean yourself up first. Get a haircut and shave. Take a shower. Put on some aftershave. Buy yourself some new clothes. Lose some weight—drop 20 to 30 pounds and you'll feel like a new man. Don't swear. Clean up your car. Be confident and a good listener. Act like a winner (even if you don't really feel that way). Be polite, courteous, and a gentleman always. Remember that girls are just as nervous as you are on a first date. If you really like her, be persistent. Before a woman gives you her heart, she needs to know you're serious. Flowers often help. After 30 years of feminism, dating is more complex than it used to be, but don't give up. Also know that many women will date "bad boys" early in their lives, thinking that their love will somehow "fix" them.

Maybe God wants us to meet a few wrong people before meeting the right one, so that when we finally do meet the right person, we will know how to be grateful for that gift.

MEN get broken hearts.
MEN feel lonely.
MEN cry.
It's not just women who suffer—men do too!

On being right: There's an old saying in marriage counseling: "Would you rather be right or be happy?" It

MEN AND WOMEN

is only human nature to want others to understand and accept our point of view. However, the more you try to win arguments with your spouse, the unhappier you'll probably be.

~ The Author

6.2 A Male Fairy Tale

Once upon a time a handsome prince asked a beautiful princess: "Will you marry me?"

The princess said, "No!!" And the prince lived happily ever after and rode motorcycles and hunted and fished and raced cars and went to bars and dated women half his age and drank whiskey, beer, and Captain Morgan and never heard complaining or had to go to marriage counseling or anger management and never paid child support or alimony and kept his house and guns and ate SPAM® and potato chips and beans and all his friends and family thought he was cool as heck and he had tons of money in the bank and left the toilet seat up and socks in the corner.

~ The End

6.3 Togetherness

In relationships and marriage let there be wide open spaces in our togetherness.

~ Kahlil Gibran (1883–1931)
(Lebanese poet)

On marriage: Many people think that getting married will solve all their problems, when, in fact, we just exchange one set of problems (the single life) for another (married life and living with someone 24/7/365). While the first six months can be gloriously blissful, after that reality sets in, and the real work begins. Marriage can be one of the most wonderful experiences possible, but each person must be loving and patient with the other.

In a marriage, there are three roles each person can play—parent, adult, and child. The ideal relation is where both people act like adults, and not like children, nor having to "parent" such a person. Marriages always start with the highest of hopes and expectations, but not all end up so well. Think of it as a garden that needs constant tending—pulling out the weeds and nourishing the good plants with plenty of sunshine, love, warmth, and water. The best marriages start out first as friends, then after that, lovers.

We all need people. It's important to be self-reliant and independent in your life, but not so much that you cut yourself off from close relationships with others. We all need people in our lives to love, and we all need to be loved by others. It is that which nourishes the heart and soul. After years of dealing with women (and a failed marriage) I finally realized I was much too self-reliant to be in a relationship—learning that when a woman loves you she needs to feel that her love is important in helping you complete your life. Being needed and wanted by others is what makes life worth living.

If you love something, you must be willing to set it free–the harder you try to hang on to something, be it love or a relationship, the more you quash its essence.

~ The Author

The ideal relationship is where a man's strengths complement a woman's weaknesses, and a woman's strengths complement a man's weaknesses. Nobody's perfect. As Rocky Balboa once said, "Me and Adrian got gaps . . . I got gaps, she's

MEN AND WOMEN

*got gaps . . . and we fill in each other's gaps." Classic.
Nobody's perfect and we all need each other in our lives.*
~ Sylvester Stallone
(American actor)

No man is an island.
~ John Donne (1572–1631)
(English poet)

Women are meant to be loved, not understood.
~ Oscar Wilde
(Irish poet)

*Love consists in this—that two solitudes
protect and touch and greet each other.*
~ Rainer Maria Rilke (1875–1926)
(Austrian poet)

Power is the greatest aphrodisiac.
~ Henry Kissinger (1923–present)
(American statesman)

6.4 Marriage

You were born together, and together you shall be forevermore.
You shall be together when the white wings of death scatter your days.
Aye, you shall be together even in the silent memory of God.
But let there be spaces in your togetherness,
And let the winds of the heavens dance between you.

Love one another, but make not a bond of love:
Let it rather be a moving sea between the shores of your souls.
Fill each other's cup but drink not from one cup.
Give one another of your bread but eat not from the same loaf.
Sing and dance together and be joyous, but let each one of you be alone,
Even as the strings of a lute are alone though they quiver with the same music.

MEN AND WOMEN

Give your hearts, but not into each other's keeping.
For only the hand of Life can contain your hearts.
And stand together yet not too near together:
For the pillars of the temple stand apart,
And the oak tree and the cypress grow not in each other's shadow.
~ KAHLIL GIBRAN (1883–1931)
(Lebanese poet)

7.0

TRAVEL

7.1 The Tourist Ten Commandments

For ten of the wisest commandments ever commended to tourists, read the rules below:

1. Thou shalt not expect to find things as thou hast them at home, for thou hast left home to find things different.
2. Thou shalt not take anything too seriously, for a carefree mind is the beginning of a fine holiday.
3. Thou shalt not let other tourists get on thy nerves, for thou art paying good money to enjoy thyself.
4. Remember to take only half the clothes thou thinkest thou needest—and twice the money.
5. Know at all times where thy passport is, for a person without a passport is a person without a country.

THE GOOD NEWS FILE

6. Remember that if we had been expected to stay in one place, we would have been created with roots.
7. Thou shalt not worry, for he that worrieth hath no pleasure—few things are ever fatal.
8. When in Rome, thou shalt be prepared to do somewhat as the Romans do.
9. Thou shalt not judge the people of a country by the one person who hath given thee trouble.
10. Remember thou art a guest in other lands, and he that treateth his host with respect shall be honored.

~ AUTHOR UNKNOWN

Once a year, go someplace you've never been before.
~ THE DALAI LAMA

Leave a little bit of yourself wherever you go . . . a small favor, a project, a gift. You'll feel better.
~ THE AUTHOR

Why travel? You'll feel more alive than ever. You'll meet more interesting people in one week than you'd meet in an entire year back home. If you can't actually travel, buy a bunch of travel books . . . read them thoroughly . . . they're the cheapest trips you can take.
~ THE AUTHOR

TRAVEL

He who travels lightest, travels fastest.
~ The Author

When visiting friends, remember that guests, like fish, begin to smell after three days.
~ The Author

When traveling, go simple. When you leave on a trip, leave all things behind.
~ St. Francis of Assisi

Only that traveling is good which reveals to me the value of home and enables me to enjoy it better.
~ Henry David Thoreau
(American poet)

Travel whenever and wherever you can. It will always give you a greater appreciation of your home place. Most people don't realize how great we have it in America, despite whatever problems our country has. Every person should spend at least six months living in a foreign country—preferably a third-world one. Europe's fine, too, but is very similar to the United States.
~ The Author

THE GOOD NEWS FILE

Try to spend a couple of weeks each year camping outdoors. You'll learn quickly how little you need to be happy. It will give you a greater appreciation of what you have at home—a warm bed, a fridge full of food, and a roof over your head.

~ **The Author**

7.2 On Wilderness

Do not burn yourselves out. Be as I am—a reluctant enthusiast, a part-time crusader, a half-hearted fanatic. Save the other half of yourselves and your lives for pleasure and adventure. It is not enough to fight for the wilderness; it is even more important to enjoy it—while you can, while it's still there. So get out there and hunt and fish and mess around with your friends, ramble out yonder and explore the forests, encounter the grizz, climb the mountains, bag the peaks, run the rivers, breathe deep of the yet sweet and lucid air, sit quietly for a while and contemplate the precious stillness, that lovely mysterious and awesome space.

Enjoy yourselves, keep your brain in your head and your head firmly attached to the body, the body active and alive, and I promise you this much—I promise you this one sweet victory over our enemies, over those deskbound men with hearts in a safety deposit box and their eyes hypnotized by desk calculators. I promise you this: you will outlive the bastards.

~ Edward Abbey

(From *Wild Oregon*, 1979)

Chief Seattle Speech

This we know: The Earth does not belong to the humans, humans belong to the Earth. All things are connected, like the blood that unites one family. Humans did not weave this web of life. We are merely one strand in it. Whatever we do to the Earth, we do to ourselves. Whatever befalls the Earth, befalls the children of the Earth. If we spit upon the ground, we spit upon ourselves.

~ Chief Seattle (1854)

(Duamish Tribe)

The New Ten Commandments

1. Treat the Land, Air, and Water everywhere as you would your own backyard, and consider the effects of your actions on all other places.
2. Thou shalt not waste.
3. Thou shalt reduce, reuse, recycle, and recover all that is bought or sold.
4. Thou shalt not continue to expect continuous growth in business and economics. Provide only what is

needed for your current population. Unrestricted growth is cancerous by definition.
5. Thou shalt not have more than two of your own children. If more are wanted, adopt them.
6. Thou shalt not litter. It is an insult to the Earth as the Garden that God intended.
7. Thou shalt conserve energy and minimize the use of fossil fuels. Try to use solar, wind, and hydro power whenever possible.
8. Thou shalt respect trees and forests. It takes ten minutes to cut down a tree that took a hundred years to grow. Plant new ones when necessary.
9. Thou shalt consider the effects of one's actions on the succeeding seven generations. Do not destroy the Earth for your children and grandchildren.
10. Thou shalt respect and preserve biological diversity and the habitat necessary to sustain it. It is the fountain from which all life springs.

The only thing necessary for the forces of evil to win is for enough good people to do nothing.
~ EDMUND BURKE
(Irish statesman)

8.0
RELIGION

8.1 One Solitary Life

He was born in an obscure village, the child of a peasant woman. He grew up in still another village, where he worked in a carpenter shop until he was 30. Then, for three years, he was an itinerant preacher. He never wrote a book. He never held an office. He never had a family or owned a house. He didn't go to college. He never visited a big city. He never traveled two hundred miles from the place where he was born. He did none of the things one usually associates with greatness. He had no credentials but himself. He was only 33 when the tide of public opinion turned against him. His friends ran away. He was turned over to his enemies, and went through the mockery of a trial. He was nailed to a cross between two thieves. While he was dying, his executioners gambled for his clothing, the only property he had on Earth. When he was dead, he was laid in a borrowed grave, through the pity of a friend.

THE GOOD NEWS FILE

Twenty centuries have come and gone, and today he is the central figure of the human race and the leader of mankind's progress. All the armies that have ever marched, all the navies that have ever sailed, all the parliaments that ever sat, all the kings that ever reigned, put together, have not affected the life of man on this earth as much as . . .

~ ONE SOLITARY LIFE

8.2 The Lord's Prayer

Our Father,
who art in heaven.
hallowed be thy name.
Thy kingdom come,
thy will be done
on earth as it is in heaven.
Give us this day our daily bread.
And forgive us our trespasses,
as we forgive those who trespass against us.
And lead us not into temptation,
but deliver us from evil.
For thine is the kingdom,
and the power
and the glory,
forever.
~ Amen

~ Matthew 6:7-13

8.3 The Eternal Truths

Practice the golden rule: "Do unto others as you would have them do unto you."

. . . Jesus of Nazareth. Treat other people as you would like to be treated. If you want love and respect, you must first be willing to give love and respect. Do this and there will be peace in the world.

There IS a God who knows and loves you and only wants what is best for you. All you have to do is ask for His help, and open your heart to whatever intuitive answers may come to you. He may not always give what you want, but He will always give you what you need. When you pray, ask that His will be done, not yours. Prayer is the act of asking God for help, and meditation is the act of waiting for an answer. Be patient and your prayers will be answered.

~ The Author

RELIGION

Finally, brethren, whatever is true, whatever is honorable, whatever is just, whatever is pure, if there is any excellence, if there is anything worthy of praise, think about these things. What you have learned and received and heard and seen in me, do; and the God of peace will be with you.

~ LETTER OF PAUL TO THE PHILIPPIANS 4:8

Judge not that ye be not judged.
(SERMON ON THE MOUNT)~ MATTHEW 7:1

8.4 Reincarnation

Stop and smell the roses now and then.

A retired teacher once asked, "How can reincarnation make sense in light of the world's catastrophes and injustice?" The simple answer is that reincarnation enables human souls to increase their spiritual development through the experience of living a long series of human lifetimes.

However, the soul needs a body to experience the ups and downs of human life that bring about spiritual progress, as seen in the results of the 15th-century enlightenment. There is obviously a relationship between our human inner selves and our souls, but the relationship is confusing at this stage of our development.

I never seriously considered the idea of reincarnation until I read Edgar Cayce's autobiography, *There Is a River*, in which he relates that Jesus came upon a blind man, prompting a disciple to ask, "Who sinned, the blind man or the father?"

(which implied that God had punished one or the other for some serious transgression).

Then Cayce explained reincarnation—or maybe it was the Rosicrucian Order or AMORC, who later explained it to me—that after we die, instead of God's rewards or punishments, a person's soul forms a symbiotic relationship with a newborn babe—and the soul enters the body of a newborn babe with its first breath of air—and (in this case) the soul becomes an objective observer of the blind baby's lifetime, where the soul (hopefully) learned to be patient, as well as also learning the value of its parents' compassion.

The use of reason and the ability to make choices are the means to achieve spiritual progress, but we are slow learners and nothing is simple, so humanity's progress requires many generations.

With the help of family, friends, and our community, we adjust to the laws of physics and nature and we learn the values and customs of our culture that are imbued with the basic tenets of spirituality—which are simply to be true to ourselves and accept responsibility for the consequences of our actions.

Except for man's ignorance, everything *makes sense* because the universe is controlled by the infallible laws of physics, which are outward expressions of an ever-present sense of intelligence. Religious beliefs are important, but their contradictions require discretion, as do different viewpoints about the purpose of our existence, such as the possibility that a

THE GOOD NEWS FILE

God-like form of logical energy has an inherent need for change—which is accomplished by the laws of physics that caused a Big Bang that resulted in the evolution of life and man's development of a spiritual inner self. Perhaps being born ignorant is our *original sin*, because all we really know for certain is that we exist here and now.

Maybe the most important thing about life is simply to stop and smell the roses now and then—and remember that God is always giving us a second chance to improve our lives and become better and happier people. God may not give us what we want, but He always gives us what we need.

~ ART CARNEY (1918–2003)
(American comedian/actor)

8.5 A Daily Prayer

Today your life holds for you endless
possibilities. You have built a solid foundation,
and you have worked hard for it.
Continue to do what is necessary to move forward
one day at a time. Write down your dream and tuck
it away—entrusting that all things will come at
the right time. Keep sight always of what is
important in life. Remember that true happiness
and purpose will be found in relationships—in the
workplace and home. Live each day open to
guidance, and your purpose will be
revealed to you. May your future be filled
with love and acceptance.

~ UNKNOWN

8.6 Forgiveness

Always forgive your enemies . . .
nothing annoys them so much.
~ Oscar Wilde
(Irish poet)

It is often better not to see an insult than to avenge it.
~ Seneca
(Roman philosopher)

The longer you carry a grudge, the heavier it becomes.
~ Thomas LaMance
(Western writer)

Forgiveness is a gift you give yourself.
~ The Author

RELIGION

*The best manner of avenging ourselves is by
not resembling him who has injured us.*
~ Jane Porter
(American romance author)

We forgive once we give up attachment to our wounds.
~ Lewis Hyde
(American essayist)

*There is no greater opportunity to influence our fellowman
for Christ than to respond with love when we have been
unmistakably wronged. Then the difference between Christian
love and the values of the world is most brilliantly evident.*
~ A Christian Author

*If you have a resentment you want to be free of, if you pray
for the person or the thing that you resent, you will be free. If
you will ask in prayer for everything you want to be given to
them, you will be free. Ask for their health, their prosperity,
their happiness, and you will be free. Even when you don't
really want it for them, and your prayers are only words
and you don't mean it, go ahead and do it anyway. Do it
every day for two weeks, and you will find you have come to
mean it and to want it for them, and you will realize that
where you used to feel bitterness and resentment and hatred,
you now feel compassionate understanding and love.*
~ Talbott Recovery Center
(Atlanta, Georgia)

8.7 Gandhi's Faith

There is no place on earth and no race which is not capable of producing the finest types of humanity, given suitable opportunities and education. I have had my share of disappointments, uttermost darkness, counsels of caution, subtlest assaults of pride, but I am able to say that my faith—and I know that it is still little enough, by no means as great as I want it to be—has ultimately conquered every one of these difficulties. I consider myself a Hindu, Christian, Moslem, Jew, Buddhist, and Confucian.

—MAHATMA GANDHI (1869–1948)
(Indian spiritual leader)

8.8 Prayer of St. Francis

Lord, make me a channel of thy peace
Where there is hatred, I may bring love
Where there is injury, I may bring pardon
Where there is wrong, I may bring forgiveness
Where there is discord, I may bring harmony
Where there is error, I may bring truth
Where there is doubt, I may bring faith
Where there is despair, I may bring hope
Where there is sadness, I may bring joy
Where there is darkness, I may bring light
Where there is sadness, I may bring joy
Lord, grant that I may seek to comfort than to be comforted
To understand, than to be understood
To love, than to be loved
For it is by self-forgetting that one finds self—

THE GOOD NEWS FILE

It is by forgiving that one is forgiven.
It is in dying that we are born to eternal life. Amen.
> ~ St. Francis of Assisi (1182–1226)
>> (Christian saint)

8.9 What It's Like in Heaven

(A Message from One Who Has Passed On)

When people die they often don't realize that they are dead and we have to tell them. There are classes to help us learn how to deal in this dimension. My body is lighter here and I do not have to eat to live, but I do anyway because I like the taste of food. It takes some getting used to.

I have a beautiful apartment with everything I need—including my piano. So many of my friends are here. I am not lonely at all.

Thanks for telling me about the light. It was very frightening in that dark place. I saw my whole life and realized where I was weak and forgot to trust in the Lord. I have been forgiven now because I have forgiven myself and so it is.

THE GOOD NEWS FILE

The friends of Gladys (the lady who died) asked, "What advice to you have for us?," and she said, "Do not worry so much. Do not strive for more money, and especially do not sell your soul to get it. Enjoy your family more. Stay true to what is important to yourself, not what you think others want from you. Love your God. I have found there are many people here from many faiths, the Catholic church is not the only way to heaven. But I am happy it was my way. I am still learning here how to adjust to my new world. I will have more to say later. Stay in touch through prayer. I miss you all and love you very much. Do not forget me. I am as close to you as a thought. Keep me in your prayers and know that your guardian angel(s) are always with you."

~ UNKNOWN

8.10 Angels

May you always have an angel by your side.
Watching out for you in all the things you do.
Reminding you to keep believing in brighter days.
Finding ways for your wishes and dreams to take you
to beautiful places.
Giving you hope that is as certain as the sun.
Giving you the strength of serenity as your guide.
May you always have love and comfort and courage.
And may you always have an angel by your side.

May you always have an angel by your side.
Someone there to catch you if you fall.
Encouraging your dreams.
Inspiring your happiness.
Holding your hand and helping you through it all.

THE GOOD NEWS FILE

In all of our days, our lives are always changing.
Tears come along as well as smiles.
Along the roads you travel, may the miles be a
A thousand times more lovely than lonely.
May they give gifts that never, ever end;
Someone wonderful to love, and a dear friend
in whom you can confide.
May you have rainbows after every storm.
May you have hopes to keep you warm.

And may you always have an angel by your side.

~ UNKNOWN

9.0

BUSINESS SUCCESS

9.1 Fail Your Way to Success

The secret of success is to know how to survive failure.

Failure is not fatal—it just feels that way sometimes! That's what I had to keep telling myself when I first embarked upon a writing career. I was genuinely astonished each time I received the standard two-line letter from an editor telling me my masterpiece was unpublishable! I became a brilliant failure, though. I was so good at failure that I finally failed *71* times before my first book was accepted for publication.

I decided that failure is not bitter if you do not swallow it. Although a failure feels like forever, it is fleeting. Each time I failed I would celebrate it as a success. *Seventy-one* times I enjoyed a meal out on my failure! I felt down each time I received a rejection slip, but I never felt out because I always ensured that at least three editors had one of my books at any one time. My chief "success philosophy" is, "Give people every opportunity to say, 'Yes' to you."

A fear of failure can so often overwhelm a desire to succeed. If you do not understand failure, failure will undermine you. We, all of us, must graduate from the school of failure if we are to gain entrance into the university of success. Failure does not stand in the way—it IS the way. Nobody begins as a success: Failure is the fire that forges the mettle in us to succeed. By learning how to fail well you learn how to succeed well. Here are some thoughts on failures:

- There are only lessons. Every event in the universe offers a teaching. Look for the lesson and then you can pass the grade. There are no failures, only lessons. Lessons are *everywhere* if you *see* them.

- Failures teach success. Every failure is a step to success if you take it that way. By learning how not to succeed you are automatically learning more about how to succeed. Every failure is a lesson in success.

- Failures are not "bad." Nothing is implicitly "bad" or "good"; it's what you do with something that makes it so. If you take it that failure is "bad," "bad" is what you get. Look for the good news in every failure.

BUSINESS SUCCESS

- Failures can be "good." Every event in the universe can be helpful if you take it that way. Defeat can stand you on your feet; endings make way for beginnings; the worst trial can set you free. Make your failures work for you, not against you.

- Failures are not final. Failure is not falling down, it is staying down—and even then all you are doing is learning another lesson. Perhaps the ultimate lesson is that you are always free in life to make another choice for yourself. Are you willing?
  ~ ROBERT HOLDEN
  (American psychologist)

9.2 Business Success

Business success: The secret to business success is to *see a need and fill it*. Look around your local community, and see what people need in terms of goods and service. Check around and see if anybody else is supplying it and, if not, start being the one who does (and at a lower price). Be computer literate and the world will open up to you. Get a website. Go to Vistaprint.com (or others) and get business cards and brochures. Four years of college are no longer a guarantee of employment, and between YouTube and Google you can learn almost anything. Specialized training (like trade schools and junior colleges) can be a great help until you figure out what you want to do. Many plumbers, HVACers, and electricians make more money than many professionals. Consider working for a large corporation for three to five years, learn their secrets, then set out for yourself.

BUSINESS SUCCESS

Once you start your business: Advertise, advertise, advertise. Give more than you're paid for—the proverbial "Baker's Dozen (thirteen donuts)." Practice UPOD—"UnderPromise and OverDeliver"—and clients will come flocking to your door, since word of mouth and customer recommendations are always the best way to expand your business. Remember that the most important customer is the repeat customer. And always save and frame your first dollar made!

On finding your passion and finding success: It has been said that the luckiest people in the world are those who really love their work. Find where your passion is, what your unique skills are, and what interests you, then develop it into a business. After that, you'll never have to "work" another day in your life. With passion in what you're doing will naturally come excellence and with excellence money will soon follow, so don't worry. Each of us is born with the potential for certain talents and skills—the secret is recognizing what only you can do. And be PATIENT in your journey!

With your job, there's always a pecking order. Learn it, work with it, and try to make your way up in it. Understanding and helping your boss achieve his/her goals is not brown-nosing, it's being an effective team member.

~ THE AUTHOR

THE GOOD NEWS FILE

Never think you're so smart that you can be a lone wolf to reach the top—you need the help of others.
~ BILL GATES
(Microsoft founder)

"It's not what you know, but who you know," is a sad but true saying. Yes, it's important to be smart to succeed but you need support from others. You may be the smartest person in the world, but unless you can work well with others and have good people skills, you'll never make it.
~ THE AUTHOR

A watched pot never boils. Do your best preparation in whatever project you're working on, then sit back and let the tincture of time kick in and work out. And, again, be patient.
~ THE AUTHOR

HAPPINESS: Money can buy you the freedom to live your life as you want to, but it won't buy you happiness. Some of the happiest people in the world are those with few physical possessions.
~ THE AUTHOR

Happiness is a direction and part of your journey, not a place or destination.
~ SYDNEY HARRIS (1917–1986)
(Columnist)

BUSINESS SUCCESS

In business, if you want to reach the top, you need to start at the bottom (i.e., the mail room). You must understand all levels of an organization before you succeed.
~ THE AUTHOR

In business, always surround yourself with the best people you can find. After you find them, tell them what your overall goals are, pay them well, get out of their way, don't micromanage, then check on their progress regularly.
~ RONALD REAGAN

Never try to do a big project at one time. Just do a little bit each day. Your intuition will usually tell you what part to do. If you're going to eat an elephant, just take it one bite at a time.

Save 10 to 15 percent of every paycheck. You never know when calamity may strike, like COVID and job losses.

It's not what you can do well, it's what you can do well consistently.

Work first: Then inspiration will come as you go along.

***Arnold Schwarzenegger's rules for success:** First, have a Dream. Second, make a PLAN to achieve that DREAM. Third, focus all your TIME and ENERGY to achieve that PLAN.*
~ THE AUTHOR

THE GOOD NEWS FILE

Any person who has drive and strength and opinions of their own will end up making enemies.
~ **JOHN D. MACDONALD**
(Author)

The squeaky wheel gets the oil *is an often heard saying. If you're having a problem don't be afraid to ask for help. However, if you're constantly complaining about things this can become problematic, since a constantly squeaking wheel usually ends up being replaced.*

Praise others in public, criticize in private.

Attack the problem, not the person.

Work smarter, not harder—and if you do work hard, make sure to enjoy your time off and play hard too.

If it ain't broke, don't fix it.
~ **THE AUTHOR**

On the birth of a new idea: *First, they laugh at you. Second, they ignore you. Third, they fight you. Fourth, they say, "We always knew that." Fifth, you win.*
~ **CHINESE PROVERB**

BUSINESS SUCCESS

*Rome wasn't built in a day—be patient
in your project and work.*

*Do your best—then enjoy satisfaction from your
successes, and don't apologize for them.*

*Have enough enthusiasm to motivate, but
not so much to turn others off.*
~ The Author

*On retirement: I take my retirement in installments.
Retirement's more fun when you're younger
than when you're too old to enjoy it.*
~ John D. MacDonald
(Author)

*Many people wait until they're older to travel and
do their bucket list only to find they have neither
the health nor energy to pursue their dreams.*

Velvet glove, iron fist *is an old Japanese
saying. Be gentle but firm in all you do.*

*Practice the KISS Principle—Keep It Simple Stupid.
Don't overanalyze or overcomplicate things.*

THE GOOD NEWS FILE

Every price is negotiable (except at Walmart). Bartering is a lost art in our modern world but a good one to know.
~ The Author

A Supervisor's Prayer

Dear Lord, please help me—
To accept human beings as they are—not yearn
for perfect creatures;
To recognize ability—and encourage it;
To understand shortcomings—and make allowance for them;
To work patiently for improvement—and not expect too
much too quickly;
To appreciate what people do right—not just criticize
what they do wrong;
To be slow to anger and hard to discourage;
To have the hide of an elephant and the patience of Job;
In short, Lord, please help me be a better boss!
~ William Davidson
(American businessman)

Philosophy of a Leader

1. Listen to your employees.
2. Provide nothing less than a 110 percent customer satisfaction.
3. Go that extra mile.

BUSINESS SUCCESS

4. Pay attention to detail.
5. Listen to your employees.
6. Admit your mistakes.
7. When you bring a problem, bring a solution.
8. Give credit to whom credit is due.
9. Don't lie, cheat, steal, or manipulate.
10. Most important of all . . . *Listen to your employees.*

~ JANE G. HOUSTON
(American businesswoman)

Would you like to know the Formula for Success?
It's quite simple really . . .
Double your rate of failure!
You are thinking of failure as the enemy of success . . .
but it isn't at all.
You can be discouraged by failure or you can
learn from your mistakes.
Make all you can.
Because remember, that's where you will find success.

~ THOMAS J. WATSON (1874–1956)
(Chairman/CEO, IBM)

Watch the one ahead of you, and you'll learn why
they are ahead . . . then emulate them.

One of the surest ways to achieve success is to observe the actions of successful people, determine what principles they regularly employ, and then use them yourself. The principles of success, as Andrew Carnegie once said, are definite, they are real, and they can be learned by anyone willing to take the time to study and apply them. If you are truly observant, you will find that you can learn something from almost everyone you meet. And it isn't even necessary to know them. You may choose great people who are no longer alive. The important thing is to study their lives, and then learn and apply in your own life the specific principles these people used to achieve greatness.

~ NAPOLEON HILL (NAPHILL.ORG)
(Author of *Think and Grow Rich*)

On retirement: Always have goals and stay busy doing things you enjoy doing. You do what you can for as long as you can, and when you finally can't, you do the next best thing. You back up, but you don't give up.

~ GENERAL CHUCK YEAGER (1923–2020)
(Air Force test pilot)

Failure is merely the opportunity to
begin again, more intelligently.
~ HENRY FORD (1863–1947)
(American automobile industrialist)

9.3 A Letter to Corporate CEOs

How do you build a successful and profitable company? It depends on a number of factors—creating an atmosphere of mutual respect between management and employees . . . and a business, where, if the company succeeds, all will profit. While making money is certainly important, it should not be the only goal. A successful business should also be one where the overall mental, emotional, and physical health of its workers is a priority. A healthy company will always be a profitable company. The following is a list of suggestions by a noted California psychologist . . .

1. Building a sense of loyalty within the company
2. Directing a *family-oriented* company with shared jobs, flex time, and onsite day care, paid leave for pregnancy and birth, paid time off to go to children's

schools to help out in the classroom and attend a child's performance
3. Making salaries equitable across all levels of management
4. Being an outstanding leader
5. Getting to know workers
6. Being available to discuss problems
7. Solving problems
8. Safeguarding retirement
9. Offering counseling
10. Creating a sense of community
11. Dedicating money to worthy causes
12. Offering excellent healthcare benefits, nourishing foods, exercise gyms, and reductions in premiums for good health habits

~ **Dr. Dorothea McArthur**
(Clinical psychologist)
(Author of *Defining Moments*)

9.4 Formula for Growing Rich

Andrew Carnegie was one of America's rags-to-riches millionaires at the turn of the 20th century. When he died in 1919, he left an estate estimated to be worth half a billion dollars.

1. Definiteness of purpose: Direct your energies toward achieving your goal.
2. Always have a positive mental attitude.
3. Have faith in your own capabilities.
4. Go the extra mile. Give more service than expected.
5. Take initiative to turn desire into action.
6. Use your imagination to seek new and better ways of doing things.
7. Discipline yourself.
8. Organize your thinking.
9. Learn from your defeats or mistakes.
10. Have undying enthusiasm to achieve.

9.5 Creativity

The man who follows the crowd,
will usually get no further than the crowd.
The man who walks alone, is likely to find himself
in places no one has been before.
You have two choices in life; you can dissolve
into the mainstream or you can be distinct!
To be distinct—you must be different.
To be different, you must strive to be what no one else
but you can be!
Find what your passion in life is,
Follow it every day and soon you can make a business of it.
Then, *see a need and fill it,* and soon the money will follow.
Find your passion and you will never *work* a day in your life.
Fulfilling your life's passion will be one of the
great joys in your life.

~ UNKNOWN

9.6 Viking Laws

Be brave and aggressive.

- Be direct.
- Grab all opportunities.
- Use varying methods of attack.
- Be versatile and agile.
- Attack one target at a time.
- Don't plan everything in detail.
- Use top-quality weapons.

Be prepared.

- Keep weapons in good condition.
- Keep in shape.
- Find good battle comrades.
- Agree on important points.
- Choose ONE chief.

Be a good merchant.
- Find out what the market needs and supply it.
- Don't make a promise that you can't keep.
- Don't demand overpayment.
- Arrange things so that you can return after a war.
- Keep the camp in good order.

Keep things tidy and organized.
- Arrange enjoyable activities which strengthen the group.
- Make sure everybody does useful work.
- Consult all members of the group for advice.

When to keep silent: Often it's best for the unwise man to sit in silence. His ignorance goes unnoticed until he tells too much. It's the ill fortune of unwise men that they cannot keep silent.

Good manners: A man should drink in moderation and remain sensible or silent. None will find fault with your manners though you retire in good time.

How to cultivate friendship: A true friend is one whom you trust well and wish for his good will. Give to him often, exchange gifts, and keep him company.

How to treat false friends: If you have a false friend whom you hardly trust, wish for his goodwill. Be fair in speech but false in thought, return betrayal with treachery, but do not burden yourself with hatred toward him.

Moderation and happiness: Moderately wise a man should be but not too crafty or clever. A learned man's heart, whose learning is deep, seldom sings with joy.

How to preserve friendship: Go you must—no guest shall stay in one place forever. Love will be lost if you sit too long at a friend's fire.

How to treat a fellow: Do not ever mock men at a meeting. They pass for wise who pass unnoticed—stay dry in the storm.

~ THE VIKING RACE
(AD 793–1066)

9.7 On Military and War

No battle plan survives first contact with the enemy.
~ GENERAL HELMUTH VON MOLTKE (1800–1891)
(Prussian military commander)

Everybody's got a plan until they get punched in the face.
~ MIKE TYSON
(Boxer)

In preparing for battle, I have always found that initial plans are often useless, but continuous planning and adaptability to changing conditions are indispensable.
~ GENERAL DWIGHT D. EISENHOWER (1890–1969)
(Military commander and U.S. President)

BUSINESS SUCCESS

In a well-disciplined army, the soldiers need to fear their leaders and officers more than the enemy.
~ ROMAN ARMY DICTUM

Take good care of your equipment, and your equipment will take good care of you. Before any battle, test all your equipment to ensure it functions properly.
~ OLD MILITARY SAYING

Engage your brain before you engage your weapon.
~ GENERAL JAMES MATTIS
(U.S. military commander)

With great power comes great responsibility.
~ VOLTAIRE (1694–1778) (FRENCH WRITER)
~ STAN LEE (1922–2018) (*SPIDER-MAN* COMICS)

If I always appear prepared, it is because before entering and undertaking any battle, I have meditated long and have foreseen what might occur. It is not genius that reveals to me suddenly and secretly what I should do in circumstances unexpected by others; it is thought and preparation.
~ NAPOLEON BONAPARTE (1769–1821)
(French military commander)

THE GOOD NEWS FILE

If you find yourself in a fair fight—you didn't plan your mission properly.
~ DAVID HACKWORTH
(Journalist)

Wars begin when you will, but they do not end when you please.
~ NICCOLO MACHIAVELLI (1469–1527)
(Italian diplomat)
(Make sure to read his book *The Prince* for a complete understanding of power, politics, money, and the military)

God is on the side with the best artillery.
~ NAPOLEON BONAPARTE

It would be a joke if the conduct of the victor had to be justified to the vanquished.
~ NAPOLEON BONAPARTE

If you wage war, do it energetically and with severity. This is the only way to make it shorter and consequently less inhumane.
~ NAPOLEON BONAPARTE

So we go on and don't do it, and let the war go on. Over a period of three to four years we burned down every town in North Korea . . . then every town in South Korea. And what? Killed off 20 percent of the Korean population?

BUSINESS SUCCESS

What I'm trying to say is, if you once make a decision to use military force to solve your problem, then you ought to use it. And use an overwhelming military force. Use too much—and deliberately too much . . . so that you don't make an error on the other side, and not quite have enough. And you roll over everything to start with . . . you close it down just like that. You save resources. You save lives. And then recovery is quicker. And everybody is back to peaceful existence—hopefully in a shorter period of time.
~ **GENERAL CURTIS LEMAY**
(Air Force commander)

The pessimist complains about the wind; the optimist expects it to change; the realist adjusts the sails.
~ **WILLIAM ARTHUR WARD (1921–1994)**
(American writer)

The belief in the possibility of a short, decisive war appears to be one of the most ancient and dangerous of human illusions.
~ **ROBERT LYND**
(Irish writer)

It is the responsibility of the victor to minister to the wounds of the vanquished.
—**DON QUIXOTE**
(Spanish literary legend)
(Basis of the Marshall Plan after World War II)

THE GOOD NEWS FILE

Both optimists and pessimists contribute to human society. The optimist invents the airplane, the pessimist invents the parachute.
~ GEORGE BERNARD SHAW (1856–1950)
(Irish playwright)

Optimists study English; pessimists study Chinese; realists learn how to use a Kalashnikov.
~ RUSSIAN PROVERB
(On the threat of Chinese influence in Siberia)

Debt was ignoble. Courage was a virtue. Mothers were beloved. Marriage was a sacrament. Divorce was disgraceful—all these and God Bless America and Christmas or Hanukkah and the certitude that victory in the war would assure their continuance into perpetuity— all this led you into battle, and sustained you as you fought, and comforted you if you fell, and, if it came to that, justified your death to all who loved you as you had loved them.
~ WILLIAM MANCHESTER
(On World War II)

If an injury has to be done to a man, it should be so severe that his vengeance need not be feared.
~ NICCOLO MACHIAVELLI

BUSINESS SUCCESS

*That city is well-fortified which has a
wall of men instead of brick.*
~ Lycurgus of Sparta (800–730 BC)
(Spartan commander)

*To be prepared against surprise is to be trained.
To be prepared for surprise is to be educated.*
~ James Carse (1933–2020)
(American academic)

*The power to cause pain is the only power that matters, the
power to defend yourself and your loved ones, because if you
cannot inflict pain on others then you are always subject to those
who can, and nothing and no one will ever truly protect you.*
~ Unknown

*Battles really are the wildfires of history, out of which survivors
float like embers and then land to burn far beyond the original
conflagration. To teach us those important lessons, we must
go back through the past to see precisely how such calamities
affected now lost worlds—and yet still influence us today.*
~ Victor Davis Hanson
(American commentator)

*I am sometimes a fox and sometimes a lion. The whole secret of
government lies in knowing when to be the one or the other.*
~ Napoleon Bonaparte

THE GOOD NEWS FILE

No proceeding is better than that which you have concealed from the enemy until the time you have executed it. To know how to recognize an opportunity in war, and take it, benefits you more than anything else. Nature creates few men brave, industry and training make many. Discipline in war counts more than fury.
~ NICCOLO MACHIAVELLI

If the enemy is in range, so are you.
~ INFANTRY JOURNAL

Whoever said the pen is mightier than the sword, never encountered automatic weapons.
~ GENERAL DOUGLAS MACARTHUR (1880–1964)
(American World War II general)

There is no security in this life . . . only opportunity.
~ GENERAL DOUGLAS MACARTHUR

Do you know what a soldier is, young man? He's the chap who makes it possible for civilized folks to despise war.
~ ALLAN MASSIE
(Scottish journalist)

If you see a bomb technician running, try to keep up with him.
~ UNKNOWN

BUSINESS SUCCESS

When you're short of everything but the enemy, you know you are in combat.
~ UNKNOWN

Every plan is a good one—until the first shot is fired.
~ CARL VON CLAUSEWITZ (1780–1831)
(Prussian general)

You may not be interested in war . . . but war is interested in you.
~ LEON TROTSKY
(Russian revolutionary)

Aggressiveness is the principal guarantor of survival.
~ ROBERT ARDREY (1908–1980)
(American playwright)

To be prepared for war is one of the most effectual means of preserving peace.
~ GEORGE WASHINGTON (1732–1799)
(First U.S. president)

We must guard the weapons with which to wage war, because the means to conduct war must be in the hands of those who hate war.
~ ADMIRAL JAMES FORRESTAL
(Naval commander)

THE GOOD NEWS FILE

Always prepare yourself for the worst possible outcome, and that way you'll never be surprised.
~ Unknown

When all else fails, read the instruction manual!
~ The Author

There is a difference between a man who is peaceful because he's been a warrior at one point in his life . . . and knows that peace is better, and the man who's never had the ability or wherewithal to be a warrior—for him there is no choice.
~ Unknown

When an officer needs to criticize his troops, the criticism is best when it sounds like an explanation.
~ Old military saying

Leaders are movers and shakers, original, inventive, unpredictable, imaginative, full of surprises that discomfort the enemy in war, and the main office in peace.
~ Hugh Nibley (1910–2005)
(American Mormon scholar)

Choose your battles carefully: *Don't waste your bullets on the trivial ones. Timing is also critical—too soon or too late is as bad as not at all. You can have the best preparation in the world, but if you move at the wrong time it can be disastrous.*
~ The Author

9.8 The Stock Market

The stock market is one of the greatest moneymaking opportunities ever created. Why am I including a chapter on the stock market when my book is about hope and inspiration? Because once you learn and master the workings of the market, you can achieve the financial independence that will allow you to pursue your hopes, dreams, and bucket list. The big money is made slowly and surely, not overnight, so beware of anyone saying they made a million dollars quickly.

There are also many stories of people making it big but who are miserable and had their lives destroyed by drugs, alcohol, or envious friends. So, if you do make it big, remember that the real treasures in life are family and friends. And, in the end, if you do make it big, know that you will be remembered more for the kindnesses and service you give to others than for the fame or fortune you achieved.

THE GOOD NEWS FILE

First, on money management—follow these rules: Pay all your bills on time every month. Second, try to set aside money from every paycheck for savings, rainy days, and emergencies. If anything's left over you can use 10 percent for fun money (or trading stocks). Avoid using credit cards, and remember that credit cards are not real money . . . they're instant debt. The more money you make, the more your living expenses may rise to consume that extra money. In general, try to avoid getting into debt. Once you've done all the above, you can consider trading stocks. In short, spend less than you earn, set up savings, pay your bills, then invest the rest.

To learn the best way to make money in the market, you need to study the great investors: Warren Buffett, John Templeton, Jesse Livermore, and Peter Lynch (Fidelity). Read *Rich Dad, Poor Dad* by Robert Kiyosaki, *Think and Grow Rich* by Napoleon Hill, *Rule #1* by Phil Town, *Money: Master the Game* by Tony Robbins, and *How to Win Friends and Influence People* by Dale Carnegie. Investing is defined as buying stocks for the long-term, and trading is usually short-term.

Never invest with borrowed money (known as margin) or money that you can't afford to lose. Avoid trading options or futures until you have at least five years' experience in the markets. Before you trade with actual money consider paper trading for at least six months. Keep a diary of each trade—entry/exit prices, dates, and reason for the trade. If you can make money paper trading, then you're ready to use real money. Always start small (no more than five thousand dollars) and learn from every trade. If you don't learn from each trade, you're just wasting your money.

Learn the difference between technical and fundamental analysis. There are proponents of both, but I find technical analysis to be more effective. Find a good online broker—like Fidelity, Schwab, or TradeDesk. Buy the strongest stocks that keep moving up. Add to your winners, get rid of your losers, and don't get greedy. Trading is actually quite simple—it just isn't easy. The good news is that anyone can learn to be a great trader. All that is required is a good road map or mentor, discipline, and some good old-fashioned hard work. Seventy-five percent of new traders quit within the first three months. Ninety percent of new traders quit within the first six months. If you can stick around long enough and keep learning, you will be successful at this game.

On the realistic side, know that you are trading against huge investment houses with megacomputers that can make trading decisions in millionths of seconds, and have billions of dollars behind them available to trade. In some ways it's a crapshoot, much like Las Vegas, so be careful. In many ways, the markets are stacked against you. Insider trading is illegal but common. However, with sufficient study and commitment to learning how the markets work, you can do well. Remember though, *the markets can often stay irrational longer than you can stay solvent.* (from John Maynard Keynes). Also know that Isaac Newton, one of the most brilliant men in history, lost all his money during the South Seas Company Bubble in 1718–1721. So, if you do lose a lot of money, remember that much smarter men than you have failed. After the great stock market crash of 1929, the U.S. was plunged into the Great Depression from 1929 to 1933. Fortunes were lost. However, 28 percent of stocks kept going up. As hard as it was to buy stocks during this tumultuous period, it was actually an ideal time to buy quality stocks at bargain prices, when everyone else was panicking. As Jim Cramer says: *There's always a bull market somewhere.*

One other thing . . . there are tough times coming for America. Our federal government spends 50 percent more than it takes in every year, like making $100,000 a year, and spending $150,000. It prints money out of thin air to cover its debt. The rest of the world is beginning to distrust us. In the end there will be a return to hard assets like gold, silver, land, water, and even cryptocurrencies, like Bitcoin. Make sure to prepare yourself.

This is not meant to be an exhaustive explanation of the stock market but it should be enough to get you started.

Here are some of the best stock market quotes from the world's greatest investors . . .

~ **The Author**

BUSINESS SUCCESS

The stock market (and the world) is filled with individuals who know the price of everything, but the value of nothing.
~ Oscar Wilde (1854–1900)
(Irish Poet)

Rule #One for stock market success . . . don't lose money. Rule #Two—don't forget Rule #One.
~ Warren Buffett
(Legendary investor)

Bulls make money, bears make money, but pigs get slaughtered.
~ Jim Cramer
(TV Host)

It's not whether you're right or wrong that's important, but how much money you make when you're right and how much money you lose when you're wrong.
~ George Soros
(Investor)

We don't have to be smarter than the rest. We just have to be more disciplined than the rest.
~ Unknown

If you make a certain type of trade and it works, make it again.
~ Unknown

THE GOOD NEWS FILE

Don't be in the market all the time, wait for proper setups.
~ Unknown

When you make a successful trade, take 10 percent of the profits and buy something tangible, like a new hat, then reinvest the other 90 percent.
~ Unknown

It's better to be out of the market wishing you were in, than be in the market wishing you were out.
~ Unknown

Spend each day trying to be a little wiser than you were when you woke up.
~ Charlie Munger
(Warren Buffett's partner)

Wall Street sells stocks and bonds, but what it really sells is hope.
~ Jason Zweig
(Personal finance columnist)

Investing should be more like watching paint dry, or watching grass grow. If you want excitement, take eight hundred dollars and go to Las Vegas.
~ Paul Samuelson (1915–2009)
(American economist)

BUSINESS SUCCESS

It is my conclusion that the successful investor must have: patience to wait for the right moment, courage to buy or sell when the time arrives, and liquid capital.
~ BENJAMIN ROTH
(Investor)

Still, let me repeat it one more time. Becoming rich does not guarantee happiness. In fact, it is almost certain to impose the opposite condition—if not from the stresses and strains of protecting wealth, then from the guilt that inevitability accompanies its arrival.
~ FELIX DENNIS (1947–2014)
(English publisher)

Two essentials for successful retirement are sufficient funds to live on, and sufficient things to live for.
~ ERNIE ZELINSKI
(Author/innovator)

It's not how much money you make, but how much money you keep, how hard it works for you, and how many generations you keep it for.
~ ROBERT KIYOSAKI
(Motivational investor)

THE GOOD NEWS FILE

If you are persistent, you will get it.
If you are consistent, you will keep it.
~ UNKNOWN

Learn every day, but especially from the experiences of others. It's cheaper!
~ JOHN OGLE
(Businessman)

An investment in knowledge pays the best interest.
~ BENJAMIN FRANKLIN
(American statesman)

Emotions are your worst enemy in the stock market.
~ DON HAYS
(Investor)

Everyone has the brainpower to follow the stock market. If you made it through fifth grade math, you can do it.
~ PETER LYNCH
(Legendary Fidelity fund manager)

Consider the possibility of being wrong, rather than right, before you enter your trade.
~ R W SCHABACKER
(*Forbes* magazine editor)

BUSINESS SUCCESS

Unless you try to do something beyond what you have already mastered, you will never grow.
~ RALPH WALDO EMERSON (1803–1882)
(American philosopher)

*Don't fall in love with your positions.
They can break your heart.*
~ UNKNOWN

*Beware the investment activity that produces applause;
the great moves are usually greeted by yawns.*
~ UNKNOWN

*It's better to hang out with people better than you.
Pick out associates whose behavior is better than
yours and you'll drift in that direction.*
~ UNKNOWN

*If you're in the luckiest one percent of
humanity, you owe it to the rest of humanity
to think about the other 99 percent.*
~ UNKNOWN

*The difference between successful people and
really successful people is that really successful
people say no to almost everything.*
~ UNKNOWN

THE GOOD NEWS FILE

Tell me who your heroes are and I'll tell you who you'll turn out to be. The best thing I ever did was to pick out the right heroes.
~ **WARREN BUFFETT**
(Legendary investor)

I insist on a lot of time being spent, almost every day, to just sit and think. This is very uncommon in American business. I read and think. So, I do more reading and thinking, and make fewer impulse decisions than most people in business.
~ **WARREN BUFFETT**

Financial peace isn't the acquisition of stuff. It's learning to live on less than what you make, so you can give money back, and have money to invest. You can't win until you do this.
~ **DAVE RAMSEY**
(American radio personality)

Much success can be attributed to inactivity. Most investors cannot resist the temptation to constantly buy and sell.
~ **WARREN BUFFETT**

Of the billionaires I have known, money just brings out the basic traits in them. If they were jerks before they had money, they were simply jerks with a billion dollars.
~ **WARREN BUFFETT**

10.0 HOPE

10.1 Adversity

*Most people suffer defeat less from lack of ability,
than from lack of will.*
~ THE COUNTRY PARSON

When we hate our enemies, we give them power over us—power over our sleep, our appetites, and our happiness. They would dance with joy if they knew how much they were worrying us. Our hate is not hurting them at all, but it is turning our own days and nights into hellish turmoil.
~ JAMES ATKINSON
(American writer)

The Lord gives us friends to push us to our potential—and enemies to push us beyond it.
~ BRANHORST KNOWLES
(British author)

THE GOOD NEWS FILE

It is only when you are pursued that you become swift.
~ KAHLIL GIBRAN
(Lebanese poet)

We are always in the forge, or on the anvil;
by trials God is shaping us for higher things.
~ HENRY WARD BEECHER (1813–1887)
(American minister)

If you have made mistakes, even serious mistakes, there is always another chance for you. And, supposing you have tried and failed again and again, you may have a fresh start any moment, so don't give up.
~ MARY PICKFORD
(Famous 1920s actress)

It is astonishing how the world makes way for a resolute soul, and how obstacles get out of the path of a determined man who believes in himself. There is no philosophy by which a man can do a thing when he thinks he can't.
~ O.S. MARDEN (1848–1924)
(American motivational author)

Yard by yard, life is hard; inch by inch, it's a cinch.
~ BETTY HINMAN
(American writer)

10.2 The Mountain of Problems

Once upon a time the people of Earth were unhappy and grew tired of all their problems, so they went to God and asked Him what to do. He said, "Go and throw all your life's problems in a big pile, then go back and pick whatever new problems you want to deal with."

So, the people were hopeful and went and did as God told them. They went around and around and around and looked at all the problems the other people in the world had. Some people were rich but unhappy and lonely because they had many false friends who only liked them for their money, and were cursed and envied by those who were poor. Some people were handsome and beautiful and successful but envied by those who were not so lucky. Some people had illnesses far worse than their own and were suffering greatly. Some people had lost their jobs and were in dire straits. Some were homeless and had neither a bed to sleep in, a roof over their head, nor food to eat. Some people had unhappy marriages and were going through the hell of divorce and family splits, some losing the chance to see their own kids. Some people had succumbed to alcoholism or drug addiction and were losing their jobs, families, and friends with only a dim future to look forward to. Some people had serious financial problems and were unable to pay their bills and were contemplating the worst of all possible solutions—suicide. Some people had been blessed with having a child, only to have the child born with deformities or incurable cancers or illnesses.

Some people had achieved success, only to lose friends and colleagues in their relentless drive to succeed. Some people had made a bad mistake early in their lives, gotten a felony, and were never able to vote, work for the government or military, have a passport and travel, or work in many jobs. Some people had been blessed with kids and a family, only to have their teenage kids spiraling out of control and tearing the family apart. Some older people were looking forward to their *golden years*, only to be in failing health and running out of money, with unsupportive kids and family, and old friends dying around them. An elderly spouse with dementia drifts slowly into oblivion—and the list goes on. In the end, everybody finally went home with their own problems.

HOPE

Moral of the Story

Your life may be hard and your problems may seem insurmountable, but if you look around and see the problems other people are dealing with, you'll realize that your own problems are not as bad as others or as bad as they might be. You end up realizing you'd rather stick with your own problems. Remember this: God may not give us what we want, but He always gives us what we need. Also, know that God puts these particular problems into our lives so we can learn the necessary lessons we need to learn from them.

~ The Author
(From my Aunt Leah)

10.3 Perseverance

Do not give up or be dismayed.
Trust in God and you will receive
your harvest at the right moment.
~ GALATIANS 6:9

Patience and perseverance; Whatever is worth having in life is worth waiting for. Adversity is never permanent, and neither good times nor bad times ever last. Life is a constant cycle between the two. Learn from the bad times and enjoy the good ones. While these bad times are hard to endure, be thankful for them, for they are the only way we can identify and appreciate the good ones.

~ THE AUTHOR

HOPE

The Patience Prayer

God grant me patience . . .
and I want it right now!
~ Unknown

Nothing in the world, however, can take the place of persistence. Talent will not—nothing is more common than unsuccessful men with talent. Genius will not—unrewarded genius is almost a proverb. Education alone will not—the world is full of educated derelicts. Persistence and determination alone are omnipotent.
~ Calvin Coolidge (1872–1933)
(30th U.S. President)

When the going is hardest, just keep on keeping on, and you'll get there sooner than someone who finds the going easy.

If you think achieving great heights of success will be easy, you either don't understand at all how the process works or you have your sights set too low. Reaching the top of any field is difficult, time consuming, and often tedious. The reason it isn't crowded at the top is that most people won't do the things that are necessary to achieve success.

They are all too willing to give up when the going gets tough. If you need inspiration to persevere, read the biographies of men and women who have achieved greatness in their lives. You will find they prevailed because they refused to quit. They continued to toil alone long after the masses had given up and gone home.

So, persevere and prepare yourself for better circumstances.

~ Napoleon Hill
(American motivational author)

I do not think there is any other quality so essential to success of any kind as the quality of perseverance. It overcomes almost everything, even nature.

~ John D. Rockefeller (1839–1937)
(American oil industrialist)

This life is not always a garden of roses. We all have bitter disappointments, especially when we expect too much, too easily. Bitter disappointments happen to everybody, sooner or later, one way or another.

The big difference lies in how we accept them. It is still possible to be happy about some things, and to reflect a cheerful attitude, regardless of personal difficulties.

How do we know? Because we've seen so many wonderful, courageous people do it.

One of the most pleasant, delightful people we know has suffered a 20-year bout with cancer. Instead of telling the world about her troubles, she gives everyone a delightful smile and takes a keen and sympathetic interest in *their* problems. Her own problems she never mentions.

HOPE

One of the most pleasant men we've ever known has worn a heavy brace on one leg since the age of nine. At times, it must be a painful and heavy burden, but you'd never guess it. He grins, passes it off, and concentrates on more cheerful things.

How can people have the courage (and good sense) to do this? I don't know, but the fact is that they do. Their courage makes them feel better about life, and makes their company a blessing to everyone they meet.

It's so important to have the courage to be cheerful, to find things to be happy about and grateful for, regardless of the bad news fate occasionally serves up.

Cheerfulness is your gift to the world. If some of the people who carry the heaviest problems can still manage to be cheerful about it, what excuse is there for the rest of us to be down in the dumps?

Are you a boss? Do you have people working for you? If so, the nicest thing you can do for them is to be cheerful and pleasant about your relationships.

It's also an approach that will win you the best possible results. A long face and dour mien will never be as effective in dealing with people as a cheerful smile.

~John Luther
(British philosopher)

THE GOOD NEWS FILE

You can reach any goal . . .
IF you know what the goal is;
IF you really want it;
IF it is a good goal;
IF you believe you can reach it;
IF you work to achieve it;
IF you think positively.

~ **REVEREND NORMAN VINCENT PEALE**

(American theologian)

10.4 If

If you can keep your head when all about you
    Are losing theirs and blaming it on you.
If you can trust yourself when all men doubt you,
    But make allowances for their doubting too;
If you can wait and not be tired by waiting,
    Or being lied about, don't deal in lies,
Or being hated, don't give way to hating,
    And yet don't look too good, nor talk too wise.

If you can dream—and not make dreams your master;
    If you can think—and not make thoughts your aim;
If you can meet with Triumph and Disaster
    And treat those two impostors just the same;
If you can bear to hear the truth you've spoken
    Twisted by naves to make a trap for fools,
Or watch the things you gave your life to, broken,
    And stoop and build 'em up with worn-out tools.

THE GOOD NEWS FILE

If you can make one heap of all your winnings,
    And risk it on one turn of pitch-and-toss,
And lose, and start again at your beginnings
    And never breathe a word about your loss;
If you can force your heart and nerve and sinew,
    To serve your turn long after they are gone,
And so hold on when there is nothing in you
    Except the Will which says to them: "Hold on!"

If you can talk with crowds and keep your virtue,
    Or walk with Kings—nor lose the common touch,
If neither foes nor loving friends can hurt you,
    If all men count with you, but none too much;
If you can fill the unforgiving minute
    With sixty seconds' worth of distance run,
Yours is the Earth and everything that's in it,
    And—which is more—you'll be a Winner, my child!

~ **RUDYARD KIPLING** (1865–1936)
(From *A Choice of Kipling's Verse*, 1943)

10.5 Inspiration

(A Collection of Inspirational Thoughts
by Various Unknown Authors)

You may never have proof of your importance but you are more important than you think. There are always those who couldn't do without you. The rub is that you don't know who.

It doesn't matter what you say you believe—it only matters what you do.

Every person passing through this life will unknowingly leave something and take something away. Most of this *something* cannot be seen or heard or numbered or scientifically detected or counted. It's what we leave in the minds of other people and what they leave in ours. Memory. The census doesn't count it. Nothing counts without it.

Without realizing it, we fill important places in each other's lives. It's that way with the guy at the corner grocery store, the mechanic at the local garage, the family doctor, teachers, neighbors, coworkers. Good people who are always *there,* who can be relied upon in small, important ways. People who teach us, bless us, encourage us, support us, uplift us in the dailiness of life. We never tell them, I don't know why, but we don't. And, of course, we fill that role ourselves. There are those who depend on us, watch us, learn from us, take from us. And we never know.

It wasn't in books. It wasn't in church. What I needed to know was out there in the world.

It's the spirit here that counts. The time may be long, the vehicle may be strange or unexpected. But if the dream is held close to the heart, and imagination is applied to what there is close at hand, everything is still possible.

Speed and efficiency do not always increase the quality of life.

Ignorance and power and arrogance are a deadly mixture.

HOPE

When a spider gets washed down a drainpipe it puts the life adventure in such clear and simple terms. The small creature is still alive and looks for adventure. Here's the drainpipe—a long tunnel going up toward some light. The spider doesn't even think about it, it just goes. Disaster befalls it—rain, flood, powerful forces. And the spider is knocked down and out beyond where it started. Does the spider say, "To hell with that?" No. Sun comes out—clears things up, dries off the spider. And the small creature goes over to the drainpipe and looks up and thinks it really wants to know what's up there.

We can do no great things, only small things with great love.

~ **Mother Teresa**
(Christian saint)

10.6 Courage

Do not fear the winds of adversity; remember that a kite rises against the wind rather than with it.

No one can predict to what heights you can soar. Even you will never know until you spread your wings.

You cannot discover new oceans unless you have the courage to lose sight of the shore.

Every job is a portrait of the person who did it. Autograph your work with quality.

The quality of a person's life is in direct proportion to their commitment to excellence, regardless of their chosen field of endeavor.

HOPE

Leaders are like eagles, they don't flock, you find them one at a time.

Your attitude determines your altitude.

Once you move in the direction of your goals, nothing can stop you.

We cannot direct the wind, but we can adjust the sails.

It takes months to find a customer, seconds to lose one. In the middle of every difficulty lies opportunity.

~ UNKNOWN

10.7 Cherokee Indian Legend
(A Youth's Rite of Passage)

His father takes him into the forest, blindfolds him, and leaves him alone.
He is required to sit on a stump the whole night and not remove the blindfold until the rays of the morning sun shine through it.
He cannot cry out for help to anyone.
Once he survives the night, he is a *MAN*.
He cannot tell the other boys of this experience, because each lad must come into manhood on his own.
The boy is naturally terrified. He can hear all kinds of noises. Wild beasts must surely be all around him. Maybe even some human might do him harm. The wind blew the grass and earth and shook his stump, but he sat stoically, never removing the blindfold. It would be the only way he could become a MAN!

HOPE

Finally, after a horrific night, the sun appeared and he removed the blindfold. It was then that he discovered his father sitting on the stump next to him. He had been at watch the entire night, protecting his son from harm. We, too, are never alone. Even when we don't know it, God is watching over us, sitting on the stump beside us.

When trouble comes, all we have to do is

reach out to Him.

Moral of the story:

Just because you can't see God, doesn't mean

He is not there.

If you liked the story, pass it on.

If not, you took your blindfold off before dawn.

(P.S. This can be for young girls as well.)

~ **Native American legend**

10.8 The Donkey

Once upon a time there was a farmer's donkey who fell into a well. The animal cried piteously for hours as the farmer tried to figure out what to do. Finally, the farmer decided the animal was old, and the well needed to be covered up anyway. It just wasn't worth it to retrieve the donkey.

He invited all his neighbors to come over and help him. They each grabbed a shovel and began to shovel dirt into the well.

At first, the donkey realized what was happening and cried horribly. Then, to everyone's amazement, he quieted down. A few shovel-loads later, the farmer looked down the well, and was astonished at what he saw. As every shovel of dirt hit his back, the donkey did something amazing. He would shake it off and take a step up. As the farmer's neighbors continued to shovel the dirt on top of the animal, he continued to shake

HOPE

it off and take another step up. Everyone was amazed as the donkey stepped up over the edge of the well and trotted off.

Moral: Life is going to shovel dirt on you. The trick is to shake it off and take a step up. Each of our troubles is a stepping stone. We can get out of the deepest troubles just by not stopping—never giving up! Shake it off and take a step up!

Remember the four simple rules to be happy:

1. Free your heart from hatred.
2. Free your mind from worries.
3. Live simple, give more.
4. Expect less—the source of most unhappiness is failed expectations (Gautama Buddha).

End of the story—the donkey came back later, caught the farmer out in the field, and kicked the daylights out of him, then did the same to the neighbors.

The REAL moral—when you try to cover your ass, it *always comes back to haunt you!*

~ UNKNOWN

10.9 Only a Person Who Risks Is Free

To laugh is to risk appearing the fool.
To weep is to risk appearing sentimental.
To reach for another is to risk involvement.
To expose your ideas, your dreams
before a crowd is to risk their loss.
To love is to risk not being loved in return.
To live is to risk dying.
To believe is to risk despair.
To try is to risk failure.
But risks must be taken, because the
greatest hazard in life is to risk nothing.
The people who risk nothing, do nothing,
have nothing, are nothing.
They may avoid suffering and sorrow,

HOPE

but they cannot learn, feel, change,
grow, love, live.
Chained by their attitudes they are slaves;
they have forfeited their freedom.
Only a person who risks is free.

~ Unknown

10.10 Today

Relax. Taste, touch, hear, see everything as if
for the first time. Feel thankful. Count stars.
Indulge yourself. Go barefoot. Pay a compliment.
Practice a talent. Speak softly. Take your time.
Let go of a worry. Take a chance. Write a note.
Return a favor. Praise a child. Hope. Play.
Relive a memory. Dare to dream.
Hug a friend. Pick daisies. Surprise someone.
Watch the clouds. Listen to the wind.
Laugh out loud. Walk in a park.
Keep a promise. Create a joy.
Trust God. Believe in miracles.
Sing. Try. Try again.
Be kind to yourself.

HOPE

Encourage others. Let love be a part of every thought and everything you do. Be true to yourself.

~ **Barbara Loots**
(American poet)

10.11 On Youth

Youth is not entirely a time of life.
It is a state of mind.
It is not wholly a matter of ripe
cheeks, red lips, or supple knees.
It is a temper of will,
a quality of imagination,
a vigor of the emotions.

Nobody grows old by merely
living a number of years.
People grow old only by deserting their ideals.
You are as young as your self-confidence,
as old as your fears,
as young as your hope,
as old as your despair.

HOPE

In the central place of every heart,
there is a recording chamber;
so long as it receives messages of
Beauty, hope, cheer, and *courage,*
You are young.
When the wires are all down and your heart is covered
with the snows of pessimism and the ice of cynicism,
then, and only then are you old.
~ Samuel Ullman (1840–1924)
(American poet)

10.12 Keep On Going!

(MORE INSPIRATIONAL THOUGHTS)

Coincidences happen when God chooses to remain anonymous.
~ UNKNOWN

If God allowed His only son to be crucified, how can we worry about our own troubles?
~ UNKNOWN

Faith is the element, the chemical, which when mixed with prayer, gives one direct communication with Infinite Intelligence.
~ NAPOLEON HILL
(Motivational author)

HOPE

*All our dreams can come true, if we have
the courage to pursue them.*
~ WALT DISNEY

The starting point of all achievement is desire.
~ NAPOLEON HILL

*Don't forget to enjoy your life while you're
waiting for your dreams to come true.*
~ UNKNOWN

You need ten thousand hours of practice to master any skill.
~ THOMAS EDISON (1847–1931)
(American inventor)

You must expect great things of yourself before you can do them.
~ MICHAEL JORDAN
(Basketball star)

*The only place where success comes before
work is in the dictionary.*
~ VIDAL SASSOON (1928–2012)
(British hairstylist)

Faith is the act of moving forward without full knowledge.
~ GEORGE GILDER
(American futurist)

THE GOOD NEWS FILE

Never be afraid to trust an unknown future to a known God.
~ UNKNOWN

To be successful you must accept all challenges that come your way, not just the only ones you like.
~ MIKE GAFKA
(Motivational speaker)

The forces that are for you are greater than the forces against you.
~ JOEL OSTEEN
(American pastor)

If you can't explain it simply, you don't understand it well enough.
~ ALBERT EINSTEIN (1879–1955)
(Physicist)

The secret of success in any venture is— endless pressure, endlessly applied.
~ MARGARET MEAD (1901–1978)
(American anthropologist)

Failure is the condiment that gives success its flavor.
~ TRUMAN CAPOTE (1924–1984)
(American novelist)

HOPE

Simplify, simplify, simplify.
~ Henry David Thoreau (1817–1862)
(American naturalist)

Why not go out on a limb? That's where the real fruit is.
~ Mark Twain

The best view comes from the hardest climbs.
~ Unknown

If you're going through hell, keep going.
~ Winston Churchill

*Success is—knowing your purpose in life,
growing to reach your potential, and
sowing seeds that benefit others.*
~ John C. Maxwell
(American author)

*All failure is the inability to adapt.
The only constant in life is change. All
successes are the ability to adapt.*
~ Max McKeown
(English author)

Sometimes the heart sees what is invisible to the eye.
~ H. Jackson Brown Jr.
(American inspirational author)

THE GOOD NEWS FILE

There is nothing in the caterpillar that tells you it's going to be a butterfly.
~ R. BUCKMINSTER FULLER (1895–1983)
(American futurist)

Religion is for people who are afraid of going to hell. Spirituality is for people who have already been there.
~ ALCOHOLICS ANONYMOUS

On succeeding at your job: Get to work before your boss and leave after he/she does.
~ THE AUTHOR

We have two ears and one mouth so that we can listen twice as much as we speak.
~ EPICTETUS (AD 50–135)
(Greek philosopher)

Lead, follow, or get out of the way.
~ OLD MILITARY SAYING

On discipline: Discipline is choosing between what you want now and what you want most.
~ ABE LINCOLN

Reputations are like fine china ... once broken, they are hard to repair.
~ BENJAMIN FRANKLIN

HOPE

Familiarity breeds contempt, so don't be too chummy. Likewise, enthusiasm should be like a gentle warmth, not a raging fire.
~ UNKNOWN

To thine own self be true.
~ WILLIAM SHAKESPEARE

Don't let the fear of losing be greater than the excitement of winning.
~ ROBERT KIYOSAKI
(Motivational investor)

If you want to make a permanent change, stop focusing on the size of your problems, and start focusing on the size of you!
~ T. HARV EKER
(Canadian businessman)

You can't connect the dots looking forward, you can only connect them looking backwards. So, you have to trust that the dots will connect in the future. You have to trust in something—your gut, God, destiny, life karma, whatever. This approach has never let me down, and it made all the difference in my life.
~ STEVE JOBS (1955–2011)
(Apple founder)

THE GOOD NEWS FILE

Successful people do what unsuccessful people are not willing to do. Don't wish it were easier, wish you were better.
~ Jim Rohn (1930–2009)
(American entrepreneur)

The reason most people never reach their goals is that they don't define them, or even seriously consider them as believable or achievable. Winners can tell you where they are going, what they plan to do along the way, and who will be sharing the adventure with them.
~ Denis Waitley
(American motivational speaker)

In my experience, there is only one motivation, and that is desire. No reasons or principle can contain it or stand against it.
~ Jane Smiley
(American novelist)

If you don't design your own life plan, chances are you'll fall into someone else's plan. And guess what they have planned for you? Not much.
~ Jim Rohn
(American entrepreneur)

If you genuinely want something, don't wait for it—teach yourself to be impatient.
~ Gurbaksh Chahal
(Indian-American entrepreneur)

HOPE

*I don't want to get to the end of my life
and find that I lived just the length of it.
I want to have lived the width of it as well.*
~ DIANE ACKERMAN
(American author/poet)

*Motivation is what gets you started.
Habit is what keeps you going.*
~ JIM RYUN
(American Olympic athlete)

*Our greatest fear should not be of failure, but of
succeeding at things in life that don't really matter.*
~ FRANCIS CHAN
(American Protestant author)

*You've got to get up every morning with determination
if you're going to go to bed with satisfaction.*
~ GEORGE LORIMER (1867–1937)
(American journalist)

*When everything seems to be going against you,
remember that the airplane takes off
against the wind, not with it.*
~ HENRY FORD
(American auto industrialist)

THE GOOD NEWS FILE

The only way to do great work is to love what you do.
~ **STEVE JOBS**
(Apple founder)

We can't solve problems using the same kind of thinking we used when we created them.
~ **ALBERT EINSTEIN**
(Physicist)

Happiness in intelligent people is the rarest thing I know.
~ **ERNEST HEMINGWAY**
(American novelist)

Definiteness of purpose is the starting point of all achievement.
~ **W. CLEMENT STONE (1902–2002)**
(Businessman/philanthropist)

Life is what happens to you while you're busy making other plans.
~ **JOHN LENNON (1940–1980)**
(Beatles singer)

*The mind is everything.
We become what we think about.*
~ **EARL NIGHTINGALE (1921–1989)**
(American author)

HOPE

*The most common way people give up their
power is by thinking they don't have any.*
~ ALICE WALKER
(American novelist)

*The number one reason people fail in life is that they
listen to their friends, family, and neighbors.*
~ NAPOLEON HILL
(Motivational writer)

People rarely succeed unless they have fun in what they're doing.
~ DALE CARNEGIE (1888–1955)
(American motivational author)

*First ask yourself . . . what is the worst thing
that can happen? Then prepare to accept it . . .
then proceed to improve on the worst.*
~ UNKNOWN

Don't wait for your ship to come in . . . row out to meet it!
~ UNKNOWN

*Aerodynamically, the bumble bee shouldn't be able to fly, but
the bumble bee doesn't know it, so it goes on flying anyway.*
~ MARY KAY ASH (1918–2001)
(Founder of Mary Kay Cosmetics)

THE GOOD NEWS FILE

I think, in a career, you have several breaks that lead to a big break. Small things here and there all add up to cracking away at the dam. Then the dam breaks.
~ MIKE COLTER
(American actor)

Be bold and courageous in all your efforts, but not arrogant. You can be strong yet humble at the same time. Be proud of your strengths and achievements.
~ THE AUTHOR

Nothing lasts forever—just enjoy whatever success you have at the moment, knowing it might end. If you're in a slump, be patient and know things will get better.
~ THE AUTHOR

Do your best each and every day with whatever you've got, then turn it over to God and get a good night's sleep. If God takes certain things away, they have probably served their purpose and He will give you something more beautiful. Say little, love much, give all, and judge no man. Forgive yourself first. Never force issues. Do not expect too much from others. Look in love and thankfulness on those with whom your karma has brought you into association. When in doubt, do nothing.
~ WHITE EAGLE
(American spiritualist)

HOPE

When life throws something at us we don't like we have three options—whine about it, throw up your hands and quit, or press on in faith. God DOES have a plan for each of us—even if we cannot see it or believe it right now.
~ THE AUTHOR

Hope is praying for rain, but faith is bringing an umbrella.
~ UNKNOWN

*Faith is being sure of what we hope for,
and certain of what we do not see.*
~ HEBREWS 11:1

Nothing gives one person more advantage over another than remaining cool and unruffled under all circumstances.
~ THOMAS JEFFERSON (1743–1826)
(Third American President)

*Life isn't about waiting for the storm to pass . . .
it's about learning to dance in the rain.*
~ VIVIAN GREENE (1904–2003)
(American author/entreprenuer)

Love many, trust few. Learn to paddle your own canoe.
—AMERICAN PROVERB

THE GOOD NEWS FILE

*The sun never quits shining. Sometimes,
clouds just get in the way.*
~ Unknown

And sometimes, against all odds, against all logic, we still hope.
~ Ellen Pompeo
(American actress)

Had to walk the rocks to see the mountain view.
~ Caedmon's Call
(American Christian band)

*You'll never change your life until you
change something you do daily.
The secret of your success is found in your daily routine.*
~ John C. Maxwell
(American pastor/author)

*There is nothing the doctor can do . . . which
will overcome what the patient will not.*
~ Your Physician Author

*Committees are, by nature, timid. They are based on
the premise of safety in numbers; content to survive
inconspicuously, rather than take risks and move independently
ahead. Without independence, without the freedom for new*

HOPE

ideas to be tried, to fail, and to ultimately succeed, the world will not move ahead, but live in fear of its own potential.
~ Ferdinand Porsche (1875–1951)
(German automobile founder)

If something were easy, everybody would be doing it.
~ Unknown

Your greatest wounds are often your greatest teachings.
~ Unknown

Where you stumble is where you extract your greatest gift.
~ Unknown

We won't be distracted by comparison if we are captured with purpose.
~ Bob Goff
(American author)

If you have built castles in the air, your work need not be lost; that is where they should be. Now put the foundations under them.
~ Henry David Thoreau

THE GOOD NEWS FILE

You never know when someone may catch a dream from you. You never know when a little word or something you do may open up the windows of a mind that seeks the light. The way you live may not matter at all, but you never know—it might.
~ HELEN LOWRIE MARSHALL (1904–1975)
(American poet)

People may doubt what you say, but they will always believe what you do.
~ LEWIS CASS (1782–1866)
(American author)

Those who can, do. Those who can't, criticize.
~ PHIL MOSS
(Australian football manager)

Health is like money, we never have a true idea of its value until we lose it.
~ JOSH BILLINGS (1818–1885)
(American humorist)

Mistakes are the portals of discovery.
~ JAMES JOYCE (1882–1941)
(Irish novelist)

HOPE

Happy? I really don't know what it is. I figure if I have my health, can pay the rent, and have my friends, I call it content. I'm quite content now.
~ Lauren Bacall (1924–2014)
(Actress)

The trouble with the world is that the stupid are cocksure, and the intelligent are full of doubt.
~ Bertrand Russell (1872–1970)
(British mathematician)

An ounce of apology is worth ten pounds of loneliness.
~ John R. Daniels
(American actor)

You must not lose faith in humanity. Humanity is an ocean; if a few drops of the ocean are dirty, the ocean does not become dirty.
~ Mahatma Gandhi

A word of encouragement at the right moment may be the turning point for a struggling life.
~ Your Good Neighbor
(Christian newsletter)

THE GOOD NEWS FILE

When you run into someone who is disagreeable to others, you may be sure he is uncomfortable with himself. The amount of pain we inflict upon others is directly proportional to the amount we feel within ourselves.
~ THOMAS LAMANCE
(Western writer)

Let everyone sweep in front of their own door, and the whole world will be clean.
~ JOHANN WOLFGANG VON GOETHE (1749–1832)
(German poet)

Be honest in your dealings, but keep your cards face down.
~ DAVE WEINBAUM
(American science-fiction writer)

Diplomacy is the art of saying Nice Doggie until you can find a rock.
~ WILL ROGERS (1879–1935)
(American humorist)

When you are absolutely sure of something, it's wise to speak softly and seldom.
~ O.A. BATTISTA (1917–1995)
(Canadian chemist)

HOPE

*Happiness is nothing more than good health
and a bad memory.*
~ Albert Schweitzer (1875–1965)
(Theologian)

*Every fact of science was once damned. Every
invention was considered impossible. Every discovery
was a nervous shock to some orthodoxy.*
~ Robert Anton Wilson (1932–2007)
(American author)

*The art of medicine consists of amusing the
patient while nature cures the disease.*
~ Voltaire (1694–1778)
(French philosopher)

*In five years from now, what will the worries of
today mean to you? Or, five years ago, do those still
affect you today? Going even further, will any of
our problems matter 10,000 years from now?*
~ The Author

*Vulnerability is the curse of the thinking class.
The greater the sensitivity,
the greater the suffering.*
~ Unknown

THE GOOD NEWS FILE

The art of being wise is the art of knowing what to overlook.
~ WILLIAM JAMES (1842–1910)
(American philosopher)

The Shell Game

*I am searching for something. I do not know what it is.
All I know is it's not here.*
~ ANGELA LANSBURY
(Actress)

Solitary trees, if they grow at all, grow strong.
~ WINSTON CHURCHILL
(British Prime Minister)

Experience is a great advantage. The problem is that once you get the experience, you're too damn old to do anything with it.
~ JIMMY CONNORS
(American tennis star)

What most often weighs you down and brings you misery is the past, in the form of unnecessary attachments, repetitions of tired formulas, and the memory of old losses and defeats. You must consciously wage war against the past, and force yourself to react to the present moment. Be ruthless on yourself and do not repeat the same tired methods.
~ ROBERT GREENE
(Author of *33 Strategies of War*)

HOPE

*Besides the noble art of getting things done,
here is also the art of leaving certain things undone.
The wisdom of life consists in the elimination of nonessentials.*
~ Lin Yutang (1895–1976)
(Chinese linguist)

*Be wiser than other people if you can,
but do not tell them so.*
~ Lord Chesterfield (1694–1773)
(British statesman)

*Simplicity is making the journey of this
life with just baggage enough.*
~ Charles Dudley Warner (1829–1900)
(American essayist)

*The happiest people are not the people
without problems—they are the people who
know how to solve their problems.*
~ Dr. Robert Schuller
(American theologian)

*It is impossible to enjoy idling thoroughly
unless one has plenty of work to do.*
—Jerome K. Jerome (1859–1927)
(English writer/humorist)

THE GOOD NEWS FILE

Priests are no more necessary to religion than politicians are to patriotism.
~ John Haynes Holmes (1879–1964)
(Unitarian minister)

He will never have true friends who is afraid of making enemies.
~ William Hazlitt (1778–1830)
(English essayist)

Believe me, the much-praised lambs of humility would not bear themselves so meekly if they but possessed the tiger's claws.
~ Heinrich Heine (1797–1856)
(German poet)

Never lend money. It gives people amnesia.
~ The Houghton Line
(Inspirational magazine)

People don't want the facts or the truth, they want to be entertained, soothed, have their tummies full, and made to feel important.
~ Dick Gregory (1932–2017)
(Comedian)

HOPE

*Pay attention to your enemies, for they are
the first to discover your mistakes.*
~ **Antistenes** (466–366 BC)
(Greek philosopher)

*There is more than one way: You have your way.
I have my way. As for the right way, the correct
way, and the only way, it does not exist.*
~ **Friedrich Nietzsche** (1844–1900)
(German philosopher)

*Live each moment completely, and the future will take care
of itself. Fully enjoy the wonder and beauty of each instant.
Practice the presence of peace. The more you do that, the
more you will find the presence of that power in your life.*
~ **Paramahansa Yogananda** (1893–1952)
(Indian spiritual leader)

*Consider how hard it is to change yourself and you'll
understand what little chance you have of changing others.*
~ **Unknown**

*When one door closes, another opens, but we often
look so long and so regretfully upon the closed door
that we do not see the one that has opened for us.*
~ **Alexander Graham Bell** (1847–1922)
(Inventor of the telephone)

THE GOOD NEWS FILE

Learning by experience is often painful, but the more it hurts, the more you learn.
~ **Ralph Banks**
(Law professor)

The brilliant man is one who improves the lives of others without them knowing about it.
~ **Dave Weinbaum**
(Science-fiction writer)

Nothing lasts forever, not even your troubles.
~ **The Builders Association**

Don't try to hit home runs every time—just be happy with singles.
~ **Casey Stengel**
(Famous baseball manager)

Accept without resentment what cannot be avoided, for it is your karma, and needs to be mastered.
~ **Chinese proverb**

In order to change, we must be sick and tired of being sick and tired.
~ **Alcoholics Anonymous**

HOPE

The faster you go, the more chance there is of stubbing your toe, but the more chance you have of getting somewhere.
~ Charles F. Kettering (1876–1958)
(American inventor)

You will never reach your destination if you stop and throw stones at every dog that barks.
~ Winston Churchill

That which is lost has served its purpose and its usefulness; something better will always await you.
~ Unknown

I expect to pass through this life but once. If there are any kindnesses I can show, or any good thing I can do for my fellow beings, let me do it now, for I shall not pass this way again.
~ A.B. Hegeman
(Inspirational author)

The greater the pain, the faster the growth. Suffering is the means of forcing the growth of the seed.
~ Chinese Proverb

As the years went by, I gradually discovered 99 percent of the things I worried about never happened.
~ Dale Carnegie
(American motivational author)

THE GOOD NEWS FILE

People must learn to gather adventures and experiences, rather than things or possessions. Possessions will burden you; adventures become memories which will enrich your soul and last forever.
~ ALFRED A. MONTAPERT
(American engineer/philosopher)

*Don't wait until you feel better to do good—
do good and you'll begin to feel better.*
~ WILLIAM ARTHUR WARD
(American motivational writer)

If you have a dream or goal, you may not know all the details of how to go from A to Z, but once you start, each detail will come your way. Do your best each and every day and God will do the rest.
~ THE AUTHOR

You can tell how big a man is by observing how much it takes to discourage him.
~ ALFRED A. MONTAPERT

The artist is extremely lucky who is presented with the worst possible ordeal which will not actually kill him. At that point, he's in business.
~ JOHN BERRYMAN (1914–1972)
(American poet)

HOPE

Forty is the old age of youth.
Fifty is the youth of old age.
Eighty is the new sixty.
~ Your Physician Author

On Having an Open Mind It ought not be so open that there is no keeping anything in or out of it. It should be capable of shutting its doors, or it may be found a little drafty.
~ Samuel Butler (1835–1902)
(English novelist)

Standing your ground is progress when you're battling a hurricane.
~ Unknown

If you can't excel with talent, triumph with preparedness.
~ Unknown

Good judgment is usually the result of experience, and experience is frequently the result of bad judgment.
~ Unknown

Do not be exasperated at the imperfections of others. They may not be as far along on the evolutionary scale as you are. Teach them what you can.
~ Alcoholics Anonymous

THE GOOD NEWS FILE

An Age-Old Truth

The test of a people is how it behaves toward the old. It is easy to love children. Even tyrants and dictators make a point of being fond of children. But the affection and care for the old, the incurable, the hopeless, are true gold mines of a culture.
~ Abraham Lincoln
(16th U.S. President)

The art of living a pleasant life is constantly adjusting to circumstances.
~ The Furrow
(A Journal for the American Farmer)

You are making progress if each mistake is a new one.
~ Edna Elsasser
(American author)

We magnetize into our lives whatever we hold in our thoughts.
~ Unknown

Instead of crying over spilt milk, go milk another cow.
~ Unknown

Expect the worst in any situation and prepare for it, that way you'll never be surprised.
~ Unknown

HOPE

Only people who do things get criticized.
~ Super Automotive News

*We cannot know heaven until we've known hell.
God created the desert so we can appreciate the oasis.*
~ Unknown

Criticism, like rain, should be gentle enough to nourish one's growth without destroying one's roots. Likewise, enthusiasm should be as a warm nurturing breeze, not an overwhelming blast.
~ Unknown

Style—the art of making trivial things seem important.
~ Unknown

*Death will come soon enough—
do not rush it.*
~ Unknown

We each have two guardian angels who are always with us. They speak to us through random and unexpected flashes of intuition and inspiration.
~ The Author

Learn from the mistakes of others.
~ Unknown

THE GOOD NEWS FILE

One stone can change the course of a river.
~ C. S. Lewis
(Irish/British writer)

*If you don't like the road you're on,
go pave yourself a new one.*
~ Unknown

*A life making mistakes is not only more honorable,
but more useful than a life spent doing nothing.*
~ George Bernard Shaw
(Irish playwright)

If you cannot convince them, confuse them.
~ President Harry Truman
(33rd U.S. president)

*It's only when we truly know and understand that we have
a limited time on Earth—and that we have no way of
knowing when our time is up—that we will begin to love
each day to the fullest, as if it was the only one we had.*
~ Elisabeth Kubler-Ross
(Swiss/American psychiatrist)
(Author of *On Death and Dying*)

*I don't envy those who have never known any pain,
physical or spiritual, because I strongly suspect that the*

HOPE

*capacity for pain and the capacity for joy are equal.
Only those who have suffered great pain are able
to know equally great joy.*
~ **Madeleine L'Engle (1918–2007)**
(American writer)

*Great works are performed not by strength
but by perseverance.*
~ **Samuel Johnson (1709–1804)**
(English writer)

*We can't all be heroes because someone has to
sit on the curb and clap as they go by.*
~ **Will Rogers**
(American humorist)

*Do what you can, with whatever you have,
wherever you are. Do your best and God will do the rest.*
~ **Theodore Roosevelt**
(26th U.S. President)

*We sow our thoughts, and we reap our actions.
We sow our actions, and we reap our habits.
We sow our habits, and we reap our characters.
We sow our characters, and we reap our destiny.*
~ **Chinese Proverb**

THE GOOD NEWS FILE

*It is a cliché to say that we learn by our mistakes,
but I'll state the case more strongly; I'll say
you can't learn without mistakes.*
~ FLETCHER L. BYROM (1918–2009)
(CEO, Koppers Inc.)

*Smart people don't argue—lack of knowledge
is the basis for most arguments.*
~ THE COUNTRY PARSON

Individuality

*Every person born in the world represents
something new, something that never existed
before, something original and unique.*
~ MARTIN BUBER (1878–1965)
(Austrian philosopher)

*A prophet is honored everywhere except
among his own hometown and family.*
~ MATTHEW 13:57

*Enjoyment is not a goal; it is a feeling that
accompanies important ongoing activity.*
~ PAUL GOODMAN (1911–1972)
(American author)

HOPE

A compliment, like a good perfume,
should be pleasing but not overpowering.
~ Dan Marshall
(American author)

One can never pay in gratitude;
one can only pay in kind somewhere else in life.
~ Anne Morrow Lindbergh
(Wife of Charles Lindbergh)

Write drunk—revise sober.
~ Ernest Hemingway

There is the Tree of Life in all our lives; sometimes
God comes through and snips off dead branches no longer
needed in our lives—it hurts initially but the remaining
branches grow healthier and stronger afterward.
~ Unknown

Everything happens for a reason.
~ Ronald Reagan
(40th U.S. president)

Follow your instinct—that's where
true wisdom manifests itself.
~ Oprah Winfrey
(TV host)

10.13 Anyway

People are
unreasonable, illogical, and self-centered.
Love them anyway.

If you do good, people will accuse you
of selfish ulterior motives.
Do good anyway.

If you are successful
you will win false friends
and true enemies.
Succeed anyway.

Honesty and frankness make you vulnerable.
Be honest and frank anyway.

HOPE

The good you do today will be forgotten tomorrow.
Do good anyway.

The biggest people with the biggest ideas
can be shot down
by the smallest people with the smallest minds.
Think big anyway.

People favor underdogs but follow only top dogs.
Fight for some underdogs anyway.

What you spend years building
may be destroyed overnight.
Build anyway.

Give the world the best you have
and you'll get kicked in the teeth.
Give the world the best you have anyway.
~ Unknown

11.0

HEALTH

11.1 Physical Health

You are what you eat.
~ OLD GREEK PROVERB

Healthy body, healthy mind.
~ JUVENAL (AD 55–128)
(Roman poet)

Secrets of good health: First, lead a balanced life. Eat only when you're hungry. Sleep only when you're tired. Always stay physically and mentally active. Walk an hour every day. Drink lots of water. Always stay focused on the positive, and do a daily gratitude list. Moderation in everything is the key to good health—that is, less is best. Maintain a good weight. If you're overweight, weight loss can solve many health problems—high blood pressure, diabetes, high cholesterol, and so forth. Lose 20 to 30 pounds and you'll be amazed at how much better you'll feel (and be more attractive to the opposite sex). Low-carb diets (as well as the Nutrisystem® program), have worked well for me. Better to lose weight than take a bunch of pills for your medical problems. The less you eat, the better you'll feel. Eating "more" food does not give you more energy—remember Thanksgiving dinners? You can also eat like a caveman—the Paleolithic diet. Think what people ate ten thousand years ago—range-fed animals, eggs, fresh fruit, nuts, and vegetables—but no sugar, refined carbohydrates, or processed foods. Also know that 85 percent of modern diseases are due to poor lifestyle choices, so always make the right decisions in your daily life. And remember, you have only one physical body for this lifetime, so take good care of it.

Health, wealth, and time are the three great things in life. When we're young, we have plenty of health and time, but little wealth. As we age, however, our wealth increases, but our time and health slowly go away. Value your family and friends—they are the true wealth in your life. Whatever point you're at in your life, just enjoy what you have and always keep yourself healthy and busy, and have goals to work on.

~ The Author

An ounce of prevention is worth a pound of cure.
~ Old Greek proverb

11.2 Mental Wellness

B*eware the victim mentality*: The minute you start thinking you're *special* (and are the only one with this problem), or your problems are worse than others, is when you start down a spiral of crippling self-pity. Self-pity is an opiate, and many people like to wallow in it. Yes, we are all unique human beings, but we are all also bound by the common thread of each of us having our own set of problems. Know that many others have the same problems as you do, so we should find solace in that. Never feel alone in what you're dealing with, and try to find others who are struggling with the same problems, like Alcoholics Anonymous.

Suicide is a permanent solution to a temporary problem: Being a teenager is a very difficult time for many, because it's the first time they experience adult problems in a new adult body. My own brother's suicide at age 33 devastated our family. Don't try to go it alone and think nobody cares. Your life has meaning to many others—far beyond what you may think. Seek out the counsel of friends, family, and professionals. No matter how bad your problems are, there is always someone else who has it worse. And never be afraid to reach out and ask for help. Like the old saying goes, "The only bad/stupid question is the one you don't ask."

On drug and alcohol use; Whatever high you experience will always be followed by a bad metabolic crash—usually the next morning. Addicts often seek that very first high but never find it again—usually with cocaine and amphetamines. Again, if you're having problems with alcohol or drugs, consider getting involved with Alcoholics or Narcotics Anonymous. These programs work, and I can tell you from my 15 years with AA and NA, that they turned around and helped rebuild my life.

~ The Author

Good music can lift the spirit.
~ Old Irish saying

On safe driving; Always assume the other driver is either drunk, stoned, or having a heart attack or stroke, and you'll have years of safe driving.

~ The Author (as taught to my kids)

11.3 A Prayer for Those Who Live Alone

I live alone, dear Lord.
Stay by my side.
In all my daily needs,
be thou my guide.
Grant me good health.
For that, indeed, I pray
to carry on my work
from day to day.
Keep pure my mind,
my thoughts, my every deed.
Let me be kind, unselfish
in my neighbor's need.
Spare me from fire, from flood,
malicious tongues,
from thieves, from fear,
and evil ones.

THE GOOD NEWS FILE

If sickness or an accident befall,
then humbly, Lord, I pray,
hear Thou my call
and when I'm feeling low,
or in despair,
lift up my heart,
and help me in my prayer.
I live alone, dear Lord,
yet have no fear,
because I feel your Presence
ever near. *Amen*

~ UNKNOWN

12.0

Humor

12.1 Humor

One day a precious little girl walks into a pet shop and asks in the sweetest little lisp: "Excuthe me, mithter, do you keep widdle wabbits?"

As the shopkeeper's heart melts, he gets down on his knees, so that he's on her level, and asks, "Do you want a widdle white wabby, or a thoft and fuwwy black wabby, or maybe one like that cute widdle bwown wabby over there?"

She, in turn, rocks on her heels, puts her hands on her knees, leans forward, and says in a quiet voice, "I don't fink my pet python weally gives a thit."

~Unknown

THE GOOD NEWS FILE

"Notice"

This department requires NO physical fitness program:
Everyone gets enough exercise
jumping to conclusions, flying off the handle,
running down the boss,
knifing friends in the back, dodging responsibility,
passing the buck, and pushing their luck.
~ THE BOSS

Whenever you hear somebody say to you "I'm just telling you this for your good," run for the hills!
~ UNKNOWN

Live fast, die young, and leave a beautiful corpse.
~ OLD ITALIAN SAYING

Noah's Ark
Never be afraid to try something new.

Everything I need to know about life, I learned from Noah's Ark. One, don't miss the boat. Two, remember that we are all in the same boat. Three, plan ahead—it wasn't raining when Noah built the ark. Four, stay fit. When you're six hundred years old, someone may ask you to do something really big. Five, don't listen to critics; just get on with the job that needs to be done.

HUMOR

Six, build your future on high ground. Seven, for safety's sake, travel in pairs. Eight, speed isn't always an advantage. The snails were on board with the cheetahs. Nine, when you're stressed, float awhile.

Remember that amateurs built the Ark...

Professionals built the Titanic.

~ UNKNOWN

An Airport Tale

A crowded airline flight was canceled. A single agent was rebooking a long line of inconvenienced travelers. Suddenly, an angry passenger pushed his way to the desk. He slapped his ticket on the counter, and said "I HAVE to be on this flight and it HAS to be FIRST CLASS." The agent replied, "I am sorry, sir. I'll be happy to try to help you, but I've got to help these folks first, and I'm sure we'll be able to work something out." The passenger was unimpressed. He asks loudly, so that the passengers behind him could hear. "DO YOU HAVE ANY IDEA WHO I AM?" Without hesitating, the agent smiled and grabbed her public address microphone, "May I have your attention please," she began, her voice heard clearly throughout the terminal. "We have a passenger here at Gate 14 WHO DOES NOT KNOW WHO HE IS. If anyone can help him find his identity, please come to Gate 14." With the folks behind him laughing hysterically, the man glared at the agent, gritted his teeth and swore "F*** You!" Without flinching, she smiled and said, "I'm sorry, sir, but you'll have to get in line for that too."

A Police Emergency

George Phillips, an elderly man from Walled Lake, Michigan, was going up to bed, when his wife told him that he'd left the light on in the garden shed, which she could see from the bedroom window.

George opened the back door to go turn off the light, but saw that there were people in the shed stealing things.

He phoned the police, who asked, "Is someone in your house?"

He said, "No, but some people are breaking into my shed and stealing from me."

Then the police dispatcher said, "All patrols are busy, so you should lock your doors and an officer will be along when one is available."

George said, "Okay."

He hung up the phone and counted to thirty—then phoned the police again.

"Hello, I just called you a few seconds ago because there were people stealing things from my shed. Well, you don't need to worry about them now because I just shot and killed them both; the dogs are eating them now," and he hung up.

Within five minutes six police cars, a SWAT team, a helicopter, two fire trucks, a paramedic, and an ambulance showed up at the Phillips' residence, and caught the burglars red-handed.

One of the policemen said to George: "I thought you said that you'd shot them!"

George said, "I thought you said there was nobody available!"

~ True Story

A Divorce Crisis

An old man calls his son and says, "Listen, your mother and I are getting divorced. Forty-five years of misery is enough."

"Dad, what are you talking about?" the son screams.

"We can't stand the sight of each other any longer," he says. "I'm sick of her face, and I'm sick of talking about this, so call your sister and tell her," and he hangs up.

Now, the son is worried. He calls his sister. She says, "Like hell they're getting divorced!"

She calls their father immediately. "You're not getting divorced! Don't do another thing. The two of us are flying home tomorrow to talk about this. Until then, don't call a lawyer, don't file a paper, DO YOU HEAR ME?" She hangs up the phone.

The old man turns to his wife and says, "Okay, they're both coming for Christmas and paying their own airfares."

THE GOOD NEWS FILE

Dear Lord,

So far today, God, I've done all right. I haven't gossiped, haven't lost my temper, haven't been greedy, grumpy, nasty, selfish, or overindulgent.
I am very thankful for that.
But, in a few minutes, God,
I'm going to get out of bed,
And from then on,
I'm probably going to need
A lot more help.
~ AMEN

12.2 Stress Diet

(This diet is designed to help you cope with the stress that builds up during the day)

Breakfast
One half grapefruit
One slice whole wheat toast
Eight oz. skim milk

Lunch
Four oz. lean broiled chicken breast
One cup steamed zucchini
One Oreo cookie
One cup herb tea

Midafternoon snack
Rest of the package of Oreos
One quart Rocky Road ice cream

One jar hot fudge
One quart whipped cream

Dinner
Two loaves garlic bread
Large pepperoni-and-mushroom pizza
Large pitcher of beer
Three Milky Way chocolate bars
Entire frozen cheesecake (eaten directly from the freezer)

Diet tips

1. If no one sees you eat it—it has *no calories.*
2. If you drink a *diet soda* with a *banana split,* they cancel each other out.
3. When eating with someone else, calories don't count if you eat the same amount.
4. Food used for medicinal purposes *never* count, such as: *hot chocolate, brandy, toast,* and *sara lee cheesecake.*
5. Movie-related foods *do not count* because they are simply part of the entire entertainment experience and not part of one's personal fuel. Foods such as *milk duds, popcorn* with extra *butter, junior mints, ice cream bon bons* and *red licorice.*
6. Cookie pieces contain no calories. The process of breakage causes *calorie leakage.*

HUMOR

7. If you fatten everyone else around you, then you look thinner.
8. Things licked off knives and spoons have no calories if you are in the process of preparing something. Examples: peanut butter on a knife making a sandwich and ice cream on a spoon making a sundae.
9. Foods that have the same color have the same number of calories. Examples are spinach and pistachio ice cream, mushrooms and white chocolate.
10. The faster you eat, the fewer the calories used.
11. Foods eaten while standing do not count—only foods eaten while at a sit-down meal.

12.3 Responsibility

Put Me in Charge

After witnessing years of welfare and fraud abuse, a young Texan lady wrote the following piece:

Put me in charge of Food Stamps—I would get rid of welfare cards with no cash for Ding Dongs or Twinkies, just money for 50-pound bags of rice and beans, blocks of cheese, and all the powered milk you can haul away. If you want steak and pizza, then get a job.

Put me in charge of Medicaid. The first thing I would do is to get women Norplant birth control or tubal ligations. Then, we will test recipients for drugs, alcohol, and nicotine. If you want to reproduce, smoke, or use drugs or alcohol, then get a job.

Put me in charge of Government Housing. Ever live in a military barracks? You will maintain our property in a clean and good state of repair. Your home will be subject to inspections anytime and possessions will be inventoried. If you want a plasma TV or X-Box 360, then get a job and your own place.

HUMOR

In addition, you will either present a check stub from a job each week or you will report to a government job. It may be cleaning the roadways, painting and repairing public housing, whatever we find for you. We will sell your 22-inch rims and low-profile tires and your blasting stereo and speakers, then put the money toward the common good.

Before you write that I have violated someone's rights, realize that all the above is voluntary. If you want our money, accept our rules. Before you say that this would be demeaning and ruin your self-esteem, consider that it was not that long ago that taking someone else's money for doing absolutely nothing was demeaning and lowered self-esteem.

If we are expected to pay for other people's mistakes, we should at least attempt to make them learn from their bad choices. The current system rewards them for continuing to make bad choices.

Lastly, I am not against all government assistance. Short-term help to people truly in a bind is appropriate, such as when a person loses their job or a family suddenly experiences the death of a wage earner. Long-term assistance only kills any motivation to improve one's life and gives the children bad role models for their own future.

~ Unknown

A lack of preparation on YOUR part does not constitute an emergency on OUR part.

~ Unknown

13.0
ALCOHOLICS ANONYMOUS

13.1 Alcoholics Anonymous

The Serenity Prayer

God grant me the serenity to accept the things I cannot change; the courage to change the things I can; and the wisdom to know the difference. Living one day at a time; enjoying one moment at a time; accepting hardships as the pathway to peace; taking, as Jesus did, this sinful world as it is, not as I would have it; trusting that He will make all things right if I surrender to His will; so that I may be reasonably happy in this life and supremely happy with Him in the next.

~ Amen

When you find yourself in the position to help someone, be happy and feel blessed because God is answering that person's prayer through you. Remember your purpose in life is not to get lost in the dark but to be a light to others so they may find their way.

One of the happiest moments in life is when you find the courage to let go of the things you cannot change.

Never think that what you have to offer is insignificant. There will always be someone out there who needs what you have to give.

Your life has purpose. Your story is important. Your dreams count and your voice matters. You were born to make an impact.

I Am Responsible . . .

Whenever anyone, anywhere, reaches out for help, I want the hand of AA always to be there. And for that, I am responsible.

Third-Step Prayer: God, I offer myself to Thee, to build me and to do with me as Thou wilt. Relieve me of the bondage of self, that I may better do Thy will. Take away my difficulties, that victory over them may bear witness to those I would help of Thy power, Thy love, and Thy way of life. May I do Thy will always.

Amen.

ALCOHOLICS ANONYMOUS

The Twelve Steps

1. We admitted we were powerless over alcohol—that our lives had become unmanageable.
2. Came to believe that a Power greater than ourselves could restore us to sanity.
3. Made a decision to turn our will and our lives over to the care of God as we understood Him.
4. Made a searching and fearless moral inventory of ourselves.
5. Admitted to God and ourselves, and to another human being the exact nature of our wrongs.
6. Were entirely ready to have God remove all these defects of character.
7. Humbly asked Him to remove our shortcomings.
8. Made a list of all persons we had harmed, and became willing to make amends to them all.
9. Made direct amends to such people wherever possible, except when to do so would injure them or others.
10. Continued to take personal inventory, and when we were wrong promptly admitted it.
11. Sought through prayer and meditation to improve our conscious contact with God, as we understood Him, praying only for knowledge of His will for us and the power to carry that out.
12. Having had a spiritual awakening as the result of these steps, we tried to carry this message to other

alcoholics, and to practice these principles in all our affairs.

The definition of insanity is doing the same thing over and over, and expecting different results.
~ UNKNOWN
(often attributed to Albert Einstein)

Seventh-Step Prayer: My Creator, I am now willing that You should have all of me, good and bad. I pray that you now remove from me every single defect of character which stands in the way of my usefulness to You and my fellows. Grant me strength, as I go out from here to do Your bidding. *Amen.*

We are all works in progress.
Let go, let God.
Relax, God's in control.
One day at a time.
~ ALCOHOLICS ANONYMOUS

13.2 Why We Were Chosen

God in His wisdom selected this group of men and women to be the purveyors of His goodness. In selecting them through whom to bring about this phenomenon, He went not to the proud, the mighty, the famous, or the brilliant. He went instead to the sick, to the unfortunate. He went right to the drunkard, the so-called weakling of the world. Well might He have said to us, "Unto your weak and feeble hands I have entrusted a power beyond estimate. To you has been given that which has been denied the most learned of your fellows. Not to scientists or statesmen, not to wives or mothers, not even to my priests or ministers have I given this gift of healing other alcoholics which I entrust to you.

It must be used unselfishly; it carries with it grave responsibility. No day can be too long; no demands upon your time can be too urgent; no case be too pitiful; no task too hard; no effort too great. It must be used with tolerance for I have restricted its application to no race, no creed, and no denomination. Personal criticism you must expect; lack of appreciation will be common; ridicule will be your lot; your motives will be misjudged. You must be prepared for adversity, for what men call adversity is the ladder you use to ascend the rungs toward spiritual perfection, and remember, in the exercise of this power, I shall not exact from you beyond your capabilities.

You are not selected because of exceptional talents, and be careful always. If success attends your efforts, not to ascribe to personal superiority that to which you can lay claim only by virtue of my gift. If I had wanted learned men to accomplish this mission, the power would have been entrusted to the physician and scientist. If I had wanted eloquent men, there would have been many anxious for the assignment, for talk is the easiest used of all talents with which I have endowed mankind. If I had wanted scholarly men, the world is filled with better qualified men than you who would be available. You were selected because you have been the outcasts of the world and your long experience as drunkards has made or should make you humbly alert to the cries of distress that come from the lonely hearts of alcoholics everywhere. Keep ever in mind the admission you made on the day of your profession in AA, namely that you are powerless and that it was only with your willingness to turn your life and will unto my keeping that relief came to you."

~ Unknown

(Alcoholics Anonymous)

14.0

PARENTING

14.1 My Own Parenting

Having a child and becoming a parent is one of life's greatest human experiences. I've been blessed with two kids—a girl and a boy—and as hard as their teenage years were, I'm glad I had them. Making babies is a blast, watching them being born is a miracle unto itself, and holding a newborn babe in your arms when they first open their little eyes and look at you is beyond description. And it gave me the understanding that being a good father was now one of my most important priorities and roles in life.

Not all young folks these days may want to have kids, thinking that bringing new life into this troubled world might be wrong, given all the problems we have. We live in a modern, fast-paced world where we're so busy with jobs, friends, family, and Facebook posts, that we sometimes lose sight of what's important in life. Hopefully you can find a life partner who values kids as much as you do.

THE GOOD NEWS FILE

From birth to puberty, they are the most wonderful little creatures possible. They are loving, enthusiastic, happy little folks who just want to be with you and sit in your lap. They're constantly asking questions and wanting to know *why*? Young moms should breastfeed so the child gets her important antibodies, necessary for their developing immune systems. Around age one, they will begin to walk and around two they discover their own minds and the word *No*. They can throw some real tantrums during this time, thus the *terrible twos*. Don't hesitate to ask the grandmothers for help and advice. Like the saying goes, *A grandmother is worth two pediatricians.*

When they're young, be careful not to spoil your child. We live in an age where "good parenting" means not to criticize one's child for bad behavior, mistakes, or poor performance. We're told that we should always give them praise and positive feedback, for fear of damaging their tender little souls. Reserve praise for real and actual accomplishment. We're also told to make our kids feel special so they will grow up with healthy self-esteem. Life is harsh at times, and we should not give our kids the impression that life will always be happy and easy. The best thing we can do is to show them how we, as adults, handle the problems that come along. They need to know there are boundaries, rules, and limitations that must be respected, and if broken, will have consequences. If they hear only positive feedback all the time, they'll turn into little narcissists and end up anxious and depressed adults. Give them plenty of chores and jobs to do, then give them realistic feedback—both good and bad. "If you want to see what children can do, you must stop giving them things." (Norman Douglas). And if they really misbehave, appropriate punishment is in order—remembering the old saying, *Spare the rod and spoil the child.*

Grade school then begins with new growth and socializing. They make new friends. Their minds are like sponges. Don't assume schools will give them the necessary teachings so surround your kids with all types of books, classical music, projects, and educational TV shows. Studies have shown that as early as six months, you can start teaching your kids about learning the alphabet, reading, writing, and even chess.

Then, around age 13 to 14, puberty hits and the hormones start raging. Girls start earlier than boys. What were once our loving little darlings now turn in to attitude-rich, in-your-face, *Why do I have to do THAT* cretins. Between the hormones and physical growth, it's a very difficult and confusing time for them. They may probe the dark side of life but remember it's just a phase. They begin thinking about the opposite sex nonstop. Don't worry about your sons wanting to let their hair grow long.

Then, the problems start—maybe experimenting with drugs and alcohol. While they may think marijuana is socially acceptable, remember that teenagers' brains are still developing and weed can really stifle and delay normal brain development. Try to guide them toward the good kids locally, but in the end they'll pick their own friends. Despite my best parenting efforts, my own daughter ended up with the worst teenage drug dealer in the county. When I asked myself the question: "Where did I go wrong?" the eventual answer was, "I didn't. She just made a bad decision." The whole teenage period is about making mistakes and hopefully learning from them. When the problems start just remember this: First, look around at your friends' kids and be glad you don't have to deal with *THEIR* problems. I once had a patient who told me that any day the local cops or FBI didn't show up at their front door was a good day. Second, when you're about to throw your kids out of the house, just pause and look at their baby pictures on the wall, and breathe deeply. Clonidine (a blood pressure drug) is very helpful at keeping your anger under control (personal experience). Third, and perhaps most important, maintain your role as their parent. As much as we'd like to remain *friends* with them during this difficult period, we need to remain a strong and consistent force in their lives. As much as they may rebel against us, they still need to know that we love and care enough to show tough love. When you give them advice during the teenage years, most kids won't say anything at the time but may thank you for it in future talks with you. It's hard to wait for those special times. However, they do come and you feel so good inside when you hear them talk about that advice again. As the sign on Abe Lincoln's desk once said, *This too shall pass*.

As tough as the teenage period may be for you, know that they will eventually mature and become more adult by

PARENTING

their early 20s. Just hang in there. Make sure they don't hurt themselves, you, or the home. Your patience during these tough years will eventually be rewarded and you can welcome a young adult friend back into your life. And don't forget to read the old story about *The Ugly Duckling* while you're at it.

A word about your marriage during this busy parenting period: Remember to still love and care about each other. After the kids come, there will often be a subtle yet real change from being *lovers* to being *parents*. For guys—know that once your wife has kids, her priorities will change and her main concern will be the kids. However, if she's a good and loving wife, she'll still do her best to keep loving you, keeping you happy, and meeting your needs. However, if push comes to shove, the priority will be the kids. It's a primal instinct, so don't take it personally.

Hope this helps.

~ **The Author**

14.2 On Parenting

Your children are not your children.
They are the sons and daughters of Life's longing for itself.
They come through you but not from you.
And though they are with you, yet they belong not to you.
You may give them your love but not your thoughts,
for they have their own thoughts.
You may house their bodies but not their souls,
for their souls dwell in the house of tomorrow,
which you cannot visit, not even in your dreams.
You may strive to be like them, but seek not to make them like you,
for life goes not backward nor tarries with yesterday.
You are the bows from which your children as
living arrows are sent forth.
The archer sees the mark upon the path of the
infinite, and He bends you with His might that
His arrows might go swift and far.

PARENTING

> Let your bending in the archer's hand be for gladness;
> for even as He loves the arrows that fly,
> so He loves also the bow that is stable.
> ~ KAHLIL GIBRAN
> (Lebanese poet)

Making life easy for children usually makes life hard for them in adulthood. Dal Smith, the millionaire founder and chairman of Evergreen International Aviation, has often said, "Thank God I was born poor, I learned how to work." Like many others who made it to the top on their own, Smith believes the greatest gift that can be given to a child is to teach him or her the value of work. It is a gift that can never be lost or stolen. It's a natural desire of parents to give their children material things they didn't have as children. Such generosity, however, often deprives children of the greatest gift you can give them—confidence in their ability to take care of themselves. When you make life *hard* for your children by requiring them to learn the value of work, they will have a far greater chance of success as adults.
~ NAPOLEON HILL

Don't blame children who are bad. Blame those who failed to discipline them. As Ralph Waldo Emerson once observed, "Our chief want in life is somebody who will make us do what we can." Although children doubtless do not recognize it at the time, they crave discipline, particularly during their formative years. Discipline defines boundaries for them, provides security, and is an active expression of a parent's love. Most important, it prepares them for the challenges of adulthood. If your childhood was less than perfect, you are in good company. Most of us have experienced difficulties at one time or another, and we all make mistakes from time to time. Your child will learn much by watching how you deal with these mistakes. The good news is that while your environment as a child will have a profound influence upon the person you become, it is not the sole determinant. The person you choose to be is entirely up to you. Only you can decide who and what you will become in life.

~ NAPOLEON HILL

Those who despair for today's youth should remember that the farmer judges apples not in June, but in October.
~ LANE OLINGHOUSE
(American author)

It takes a village to raise a child—parents, siblings. grandparents, neighbors, aunts and uncles, teachers, strangers, mailmen, random encounters, sports, cousins, family friends, school, travel, and so on. Each encounter can bring lessons and understanding—both good and bad.
~ OLD AMERICAN SAYING

14.3 Things Our Parents Meant to Tell Us but Couldn't Always Find the Words

1. Give people more than they expect and do it cheerfully.
2. Don't believe all you hear—especially on TV and the media.
3. When you say, "I love you," mean it.
4. Be engaged at least a year before you get married (see 5).
5. Believe in love at first sight but remember that it takes at least a year to really get to know somebody.
6. Never laugh at anyone's dreams.
7. Love deeply and passionately. You might get hurt but it's the only way to live life completely.

8. In disagreements, fight fairly. No name calling. Stay focused on the current situation and don't bring up the past.
9. Don't judge people by their relatives.
10. Talk slowly but think quickly. Don't be afraid to say *No* if it doesn't feel right.
11. When someone asks you a question, and you don't want to answer, smile and ask, "Why do you want to know?"
12. Remember that great love and great achievements involve great risk.
13. Call your dad and mom.
14. When you make a promise, keep it.
15. Remember the three Rs; Respect for self, Respect for others, Responsibility for all your actions.
16. Don't let a little dispute injure a great friendship.
17. When you realize you've made a mistake, take immediate steps to correct it.
18. Marry a man/woman you like to talk to. Most relationships start with physical attraction but that cools off after the first few months, so it's important to be friends first, then lovers second.
19. Read more books, and watch less TV.
20. Live a good and honorable life—then when you get older and think back, you'll get to enjoy it a second time.
21. Trust in God but lock your car.

PARENTING

22. Share your knowledge. It's a way to achieve immortality.
23. Never interrupt someone when you're being flattered.
24. Mind your own business. Help others only when they ask for it.
25. Remember that not getting what you want is sometimes a stroke of luck. Know also that when one door closes, another one always opens, so don't panic, wait a bit, and see what new opportunities arise.
26. To get love, you must first be willing to give love.
27. Judge your success by what you had to give up to get it.
28. Remember that your character is your destiny.

~ UNKNOWN

15.0

FINAL THOUGHTS

15.1 Believe in Yourself

Believe in yourself: The only limit to your success in life is the limit you place on yourself. And other people need to believe in you as well. As John D. MacDonald (author) says, "Somebody has to believe in you all the way. You have to be important to somebody, or life is just a routine of going through the motions."

Patience: Patience is not the absence of action, but the timing of one's action. Patience waits for the right time to act. Define what your goals are, do your best to prepare for these goals, then wait for the window of opportunity to open. As Rev. Fulton J. Sheen once said, "Timing is everything." As the Bible says, "Good things come to those who wait." And, when opportunity does come, remember that fortune favors the bold.

THE GOOD NEWS FILE

Be prepared: As an Eagle Scout, this was the most important rule I learned. Look into your future and see what may be coming your way. No need to worry about the future if you take steps to prepare for it. If you see a storm coming, buy a raincoat.

Motion: Never confuse motion with progress or achievement. Many people are constantly busy but never really achieve anything. Always have a one- and five-year plan. A one-year plan for short-term goals, and a five-year for bigger goals. If you don't have goals, you just bounce from one random event to another. A ship without a rudder will just drift endlessly. Always have a goal and project to work on.

Adaptability: The only constant in life is change and the only way to survive is to be able to adapt to whatever life throws at you.

Carpe diem: *Carpe diem* means *seize the day* in Latin. Live each day to the fullest and as if it were your last. Do nothing dangerous, but don't waste your precious time. Life is a God-given gift and must not be squandered. The things people often regret at the end of life are not the things they've done, but often the things they wished they'd done.

Do your best: At the end of each day, when dealing with whatever problems you have—just ask yourself, "Did I do

FINAL THOUGHTS

the best with whatever I've got?" If the answer is yes, then rest easy and sleep well. Tomorrow is always another day and another chance to keep on living.

Failure and mistakes: As Malcolm Forbes says, "Failure is success if we learn from it." Failure and making mistakes show that you are at least trying to move forward. Any lessons learned will move us toward improvement and perfection. Just don't make the same mistakes twice; otherwise, it's a wasted experience and you're not paying attention. Mistakes are part of the learning process and the portals of discovery. Those who fail to learn the lessons of history are doomed to repeat them.

Thought: You always become what you think most about. Whatever you create in your mind, and want passionately, will eventually become physical reality. As John D. McDonald (author) says, "Think of something hard enough and long enough and it happens every time." And good thoughts will attract other good thoughts, and bad thoughts only negative ones.

~ The Author

Activism: What's the best way to be an activist for liberty? Find the thing you do best, whatever it is, in any sector of life—and do it in a way that strives for excellence in the service of yourself, those you love, and the relevant social unit that is affected by your work. A life well lived serves the cause of liberty better than any other path.

~ Jeffrey Tucker
(American economics writer)

Politics, religion, and sex: Never discuss these three subjects—they will always bring arguments and disagreements between people—even among friends. Try to avoid them, unless you like to argue.

No: Never be afraid to say the word *no*. It can save you massive time, stress, and headaches.

Power, money, and sex: To understand any situation, follow the flow (and origin) of these three. These three have always ruled the world (along with love and kindness). Once you understand how people are getting motivated by these things you can understand what's really going on. Know also there's a darker side of life where bribes, threats, and doing favors often rule the game. Wealthy people know that everybody *has a price*—a high price where they might do something they wouldn't normally do. Also, never threaten the money flow in your job (like criticizing your superiors), or you may end up losing it (or worse).

Listening: If you want to make friends, be a good listener. The more you listen, the more you learn. And the

FINAL THOUGHTS

more you listen, the smarter people will think you are (for some unknown reason). As Alcoholics Anonymous says, "Take the cotton out of your ears, and put it in your mouth."

Criticism: As Michelangelo once said, "Criticize by creating." If you're going to criticize something, always have a better solution to offer for the problem.

Life: Life is a marathon, not a sprint, so pace yourself. Work hard but also take time to play, relax, and enjoy the good things along the way. Success is a journey, not a destination. Happiness is a direction and part of your journey, not a place.

Kindness: Human kindness always goes a long way and works better than force.

Reading: Read, read, and read some more. Read all the books you can throughout your life. Reading can take you on adventures of the mind and soul while sitting in the comfort of your home.

~ THE AUTHOR

Being broke is temporary . . . being poor is a state of mind.
~ MIKE TODD (1909–1958)
(TV producer)

THE GOOD NEWS FILE

Courtesy: Be gentle, courteous, and humble but tough and alert as well. It is always necessary to stay strong but do it in an effective manner. As Teddy Roosevelt once said, "Walk softly but carry a big stick." Your actions will always speak louder than your words.

~ The Author

About the Author

Dr. D. Lynn Mickleson was born in 1950 and raised in a steel town in western Pennsylvania. Blessed with a loving and supportive family he was able to achieve many of the goals in his early life. He earned his Eagle Scout award at age 14 and continued to use the important concepts he learned in scouting throughout his adult life. Service to others has always been his main goal—first in medicine, then in teaching others about the importance of hope and inspiration.

He graduated from Dickinson College in 1972 (BS-Biology) then spent five years working as a boatman on the Colorado River, managing an apartment, working in the Post Office and doing graduate work in Physiology at Penn State. Finally, after five years of medical school rejections (51 in total), he was accepted to Temple Medical School and graduated with his MD in 1981. After that he received specialty training in Emergency Medicine. From 1984–87 he served as a US Navy Flight Surgeon at NAS Key West. In 1990 he moved his family to Palmer, Alaska where he has lived since. After his ER career he had his own practice in Palmer for many years.

As a world traveler he's been to Europe, Nepal, Scandinavia, and Central and South America. Everywhere he's gone he's found stories of hope, inspiration and the perseverance of the human spirit over high odds.

Early in his life he learned the power of positive thinking from such luminaries as Norman Vincent Peale, Dale Carnegie, Napoleon Hill and Reverend Robert Schuller. He realized that both good and bad things happen to all of us on a regular basis. When something good happens we feel happy for a short while then our minds drift back to the more painful problems in our lives. He then realized he needed to write these good things down or he would forget them. Thus was born the concept of the Good News File.

Over the past 50 years he has collected thousands of inspirational quotes and stories from many sources. It became clear there was a real need to put them all in a book to help people in these difficult times . . . thus began the book "The Good News File—Hope For A Modern World."

Enjoy the book.

Acknowledgments

As a first-time author wanting to self-publish, it was a challenge to find a non-traditional publisher who could walk me through the long and complex process of putting together a quality book. After querying over a dozen publishers, I was fortunate to find Michele DeFilippo and her excellent team at 1106 Design in Arizona.

Writing a book has many steps–writing your first draft, having it professionally edited, formatting, reviewing by a proofreader, setting up a website, designing a cover, getting it on Amazon and Ingram, and finding a quality printer. It's a lot like a general contractor building a house who then subcontracts all the parts like carpentry, roofing, etc. Many authors try to do it on their own but only end up with a sub-standard book and having to deal with multiple different businesses. The beauty of 1106 Design is that all these services are under one roof. Their prices are reasonable and fixed, so there are no surprises. They can also help with marketing your book, which is the second and perhaps most important part of your book project.

Special thanks to Ronda Rawlins, who was a constant source of help and encouragement, Bob for his proofreading, Jerome for website development, and others who were all part of the effort. If I had a nickel for every time I felt like giving up (especially as an older guy who is computer-challenged), I'd be a rich man. Without 1106's help, I could not have done it.

Many thanks also to my loving and supportive family and friends who offered constant help throughout this book project, as well as my colleagues in Alcoholics Anonymous. We are all on a journey of learning, healing, and soul development. There IS a God who knows and loves each and every one of us and all we have to do is ask for His help.

This has been a labor of love for me, and hopefully, you'll enjoy the book. It's been a lot of work, but in the end, you can get your message out there to the world. If you feel you have a book within you, then start now and don't wait.

Thank you for reading and I hope you enjoyed this book. Would you do me a favor?

Like all authors, I rely on online reviews to encourage future sales. Your opinion is invaluable. Would you take a few moments now to share your assessment of my book at the online review site of your choice? Your opinion will help the book marketplace become more transparent and useful to all.

Thank you very much!

www.ingramcontent.com/pod-product-compliance
Lightning Source LLC
Chambersburg PA
CBHW071802080526
44589CB00012B/652